MW01670903

Fundamentals Of SPIRITUAL WARFARE

A Believer's Guide to Overcoming the Enemy

Terry S. Wise, Ph.D.

SIMON & SCHUSTER CUSTOM PUBLISHING

Cover design: Alyssa Yesh

Copyright © 1996 Terry S. Wise.
All rights reserved.

Permission in writing must be obtained from the publisher before any part of this work may be reproduced or transmitted in any form or by any means, electronic or mechanical, including photocopying and recording, or by any information storage or retrieval system.

Printed in the United States of America

10 9 8 7 6 5 4 3 2 1

ISBN 0–536–59440-6
BA 96030

SIMON & SCHUSTER CUSTOM PUBLISHING
160 Gould Street/Needham Heights, MA 02194
Simon & Schuster Education Group

COPYRIGHT ACKNOWLEDGMENTS

Grateful acknowledgment is made to the following sources for permission to reprint material copyrighted or controlled by them:

Unless otherwise noted, all Scripture quotations are taken from *New American Standard Bible*. Copyright © 1960, 1962, 1963, 1968, 1971, 1972, 1973, 1975, 1977 by The Lockman Foundation. Used by permission.

Scripture quotations marked NIV are taken from the *Holy Bible,* New International Version. Copyright © 1973, 1978, 1984 by the International Bible Society. Used by permission of Zondervan Bible Publishers.

Scripture quotations marked KJV are taken from the *Holy Bible,* New King James Version. Copyright © 1979, 1980, 1982 by Thomas Nelson, Inc. Used by permission. All rights reserved.

Dedication

To my wife, Judy,
and to our children
Elliott and Natalie

I love you more than
words can express.
You are my best
friends and truly
God's gifts to me!

CONTENTS

	INTRODUCTION	11
1	SATAN'S PREDICAMENT	21
2	FOUNDATIONAL ISSUES	35
3	DEMON POSSESSION	51
4	STRATEGIC BATTLEFIELDS	73
5	THE ARMOR OF GOD	99
6	PRAYER, THE ULTIMATE WARFARE WEAPON	111
7	POWER, TRUTH, AND AUTHORITY	127
8	STEPS TO FREEDOM	139
9	BEGINNING A FREEDOM MINISTRY	173
	Appendix	183
	Notes	193
	Selected Bibliography	195

PREFACE

I have been frustrated with the incongruity between the victory we are supposed to experience and the defeated life we actually live. Christians often function in survival mode on a daily basis. They barely squeeze out another day of Christian existence while being bombarded by the enemy and defeated in their faith.

When we are deceived about Satan's deceptive strategies in our life, we remain in this meager Christian existence never really doing much for God and never too much of a threat to Satan. This book exposes the devil's covert activities and charts a biblical path to victory.

The time is ripe for heightened levels of awareness and a new movement among God's people for advancing His kingdom. Far from being drenched in the sensationalism that often surrounds the topic, this book emphasizes the truth of Scripture and contains a biblical, rational, and powerful approach for overcoming the enemy. If you are tired of defeat and desire to move on to victorious Christian living, then this book is for you. It will help you:

- Discover Satan's awful predicament.
- Expose Satan's deceptive strategies.
- Counter Satan's lies with God's truth.
- Learn why Satan attacks Christians.
- Harness your thought life under the Holy Spirit's control.
- Implement your delegated authority in Christ.
- Understand and utilize the armor of God.
- Gain a fresh realization of the power of prayer.
- Find freedom from demonic bondage.
- Lead others to freedom in Christ.

Many are sensing a level of victory never before experienced because they have learned to expose and confront Satan's deceptive schemes in their life. It is time to take a stand against the enemy and begin living a life of victory. After all, if God is for us, who can be against us? (Rom. 8:31).

Acknowledgements

Deep gratitude is extended to my Heavenly Father. Without the death and resurrection of Jesus Christ there would be no victory over the enemy and no need for a book on spiritual warfare.

The writing of this book has seen the burning of midnight oil on more occasions than I can count. My family has not only allowed me time to complete this work, but they even helped edit the material. I will miss the special hugs and kisses I received while typing at the computer. Thank you Judy, Elliott, and Natalie.

A special thanks is extended to the staff and faculty of Trinity College and Theological Seminary for allowing me to teach on this important topic. It is a privilege to work with each of you.

I am grateful to Simon & Schuster for publishing an evangelical approach to spiritual warfare. David Daniels, my editor, has been both a friend and a helpful guide throughout the process.

INTRODUCTION

The redeemed children of God are more than an audience on a Sunday morning, they are an army, advancing the Kingdom of God under the authority and banner of Jesus Christ. Christianity is not a spectator sport. No one is to sit on the sideline.

The sleeping bag became my security blanket as amazing missionary stories filled the midnight air. Feeling both scared and excited, my first introduction to spiritual warfare came while I was a young man at Bible camp. My cabin counselor, a former missionary to Indonesia, captured my attention with such tales as the brutal stabbing of a young female missionary, and God's wondrous protection during an Indonesian coup attempt.

But it was the stories of demonic activity that mesmerized me. In sharp contrast to the fanciful myths often invented by camp counselors to scare gullible campers, these stories were absolutely true and real!

Limiting these accounts to Indonesia would have helped me sleep better, but the counselor also recited activities very close to home like ministering to a demonically oppressed teenager while counseling at another camp.

In another story, he told of a man who became upset during a counseling session. The demonic powers evident in the actions and behaviors of the counselee were undeniable. After knocking him out of his chair, the counselee lifted a large rock high above his head in an effort to crush the counselor. The counselor cried out, "In the name of Jesus Christ, I command you to turn around immediately and walk out that front door." In complete submission to this authoritative command, the man did just that.

These first remembrances of spiritual warfare quickly convinced me that there really was something to this subject. I may not have understood the topic very well at that time, but I did comprehend its reality and power.

The Reality of Spiritual Warfare

There are those today who do not believe in the existence of Satan and demons. Others readily assent to a theological position about Satan (that he exists and is corrupt), but falter when it comes to the practical application of spiritual warfare to their own lives. A theology that does not impact the way one lives, acts, and reacts, is absolutely worthless.

Whether we realize it or not, Satan is doing all he can to thwart our efforts to live holy lives which honor God and produce spiritual impact. It is pure naiveté to believe that once we become Christians, we are no longer attacked, buffeted, and challenged by Satan and his cohorts.

Ephesians 6:12 plainly states, "For our struggle is not against flesh and blood, but against the rulers, against the powers, against the world forces of this darkness, against the spiritual forces of wickedness in the heavenly places." The word "struggle," from the Greek root "pallo," literally means "to swing round, sway backward and forward," and creates the mental image of a struggle or wrestling match taking place.

In the contemporary church environment, Christians often fight more with one another than with their true enemy, the devil. Satan is delighted with any activity which promotes division and redirects the focus from himself. If believers are not involved in spiritual warfare, why would Paul go to the trouble of describing our protective gear and exhorting us to "take up" and "put on" the "full armor of God?"

In another powerfully descriptive verse, 1 Peter 5:8 adds, "Be of sober spirit, be on the alert. Your adversary, the devil, prowls about like a roaring lion, seeking someone to devour." One of the obvious reasons we are to "be of sober spirit" and "on the alert" is the reality of an evil enemy, Satan. Both words, "adversary" and "devil," suggest a malicious foe seeking to devour Christians as a lion devours its prey.

Peter does not say that Satan "prowls about like a squeaky mouse, seeking someone to devour." The likeness to a ferocious lion informs us that we face a formidable opponent. Although Satan is a defeated foe, he cannot be taken lightly. His ferocious nature prompts us to be alert and of sober spirit toward his evil and deceptive schemes.

Referring to one particular warfare tactic, James 4:7 says, "Submit therefore to God. Resist the devil and he will flee from you." If Satan is not attacking and oppressing Christians, why would we be asked to resist? Scripture portrays a literal enemy who should be taken very seriously.

No Exemptions From the Army

Becoming a Christian does not exempt one from spiritual warfare. Quite the opposite is true! Christians are drafted into God's army at the moment of conversion. Their military assignment is to pillage and plunder enemy strongholds, releasing those whom Satan holds as prisoners to sin (Mt. 12:29; 28:18-20; Lk. 10:19). As one drill sergeant said to new recruits, "Welcome to the Army!"

The redeemed children of God are more than an audience on a Sunday morning, they are an army, advancing the Kingdom of God under the authority and banner of Jesus Christ. Christianity is not a spectator sport. No one is to sit on the sideline.

Excessive Interest and Blatant Disbelief

Knowing full well what damage properly trained personnel in God's military can inflict, Satan attempts, in any way possible, to confuse individuals by clouding the subject with controversy, stirring up unfounded fear, and promoting extreme approaches.

C.S. Lewis once wrote, "There are two equal and opposite errors into which our race can fall about the devils. One is to disbelieve in their existence. The other is to believe, and to feel an excessive and unhealthy interest in them. They themselves are equally pleased by both errors and hail a materialist or a magician with the same delight."[1]

There are those, and I have met many of them, whose "Ghost Buster" mentality plunges them into a God-squad demon hit team. They spend their time looking for individuals who might need their expert exorcism techniques. For them, demons are behind every problem, such as the demon of financial trouble, the demon of sunburn, the demon of lust, etc. You name it, there is a demon for it!

Their motives may be pure, but zeal without knowledge can easily lead one astray. Others use the "demons behind every bush" hypothesis as a scapegoat. By preoccupying themselves with this subject, they banish from their priority list those issues in their own life which require discipline, training, and critical thinking.

Like a cocaine addict longing for that next hit, "Ghost Busters" receive their spiritual high through a fixation on demons. It makes them feel important, needed, and close to the reality of spiritual dimensions. However, one is completely out of balance when the pendulum swings too far this way.

On the extreme opposite side of the pendulum are those who deny the existence of a real devil. For them, believing in a literal, personal devil is to regress into unenlightened times. Since we live in a high-tech, modern era, with medical, technological, and scientific advances which confound the mind, how could one possibly believe in a little red devil with horns, pitchfork, and cloven hoofs?

Interestingly enough, this view occurs mainly in areas where Christianity already exists. Could we have become immune to our own teaching? Other, less advanced cultures, have no trouble believing in the existence and power of an evil being. Familiarity with Christianity may have brought about a smug sophistication which says, "We are far too smart to believe that!"

Though the world has progressed technologically and scientifically over the years, God and Satan have not changed. What was true about them thousands of years ago is still true of them today. God is still on His glorious throne and Satan is still up to his evil schemes.

Culture is to be interpreted though the Bible. Interpreting the Bible through the grid of current culture is backwards. If current culture becomes the standard for interpreting and understanding the biblical record, then everything is relative. When culture changes, the meaning of the Bible changes. Besides, which culture should be used as the standard for interpretation?

This approach to Scripture ultimately leads to faulty conclusions and a false sense of security. Satan is delighted when individuals dismiss him, ridicule him, forget about him, underestimate him, or soft-pedal the power of the Cross. When this occurs, he accomplishes his nasty work without the restraining force of powerful Christians in the regiments of God.

Balance is the key. Understanding who Satan is, what he tries to do, and how he goes about accomplishing his goals, helps us to stand victoriously against him. Balance says, "Yes, Satan is working against me, but not everything is a direct assault from him. I am able to conquer the devil through the power of the finished work of Calvary and my new identity as a redeemed child of God."

This world is experiencing increased overt activity in witchcraft, the New Age movement, eastern religious teachings, occult involvement, immorality, violence, and the like. Satan is on the move to affect the mental, physical, and spiritual welfare of Christians. As we move closer toward the end times, and the battle intensifies, each of us must be more prepared than ever!

Missionaries and Spiritual Warfare

Spiritual warfare is also a topic of special significance to missionaries. Many of the unreached people groups in the world today have a strong belief that spirit power permeates everything that is and everything that happens in the world. There is a desire to interact with this power, and ultimately control it.

The following missionary report conveys the struggle missionaries often face:

> *His eyes were glassy, his clothes ragged, his hair matted, and he was desperate. "I'm going to kill this animal," he repeated three times. I thought he was talking about me.*

The lady of the house gave us all some strong coffee, but he didn't want it. Suddenly he fell on the floor, knocking the dishes off the table. As we dragged him out of the house, he looked up at me and said, "Have mercy on me," then I recognized his problem. He was demon possessed. These spells began after he stopped attending an evangelical church and turned to spiritism.

I remembered the words of Jesus. "Behold, I give you [authority] over all the power of the enemy, and nothing by any means shall hurt you." I felt I should rebuke the demon in the name of Jesus, but what if nothing happened? All the people gathered would ridicule me...

There I was, a defeated missionary in the interior of Brazil, ready to pack up and go home. When face to face with the enemy, I was afraid.[2]

Missionaries often go into the field with little or no training in spiritual warfare. Seminaries and missionary training centers often exclude the study of this crucial aspect of successful Christian living. Conversations with missionaries during church mission conferences will provide plentiful stories of warfare encounters. Unfortunately, many of them do not end in victory. The essential training in spiritual warfare was somehow neglected along the way.

Ministering to Others

It is my sincere hope that this book will be of great value to those desiring to make a significant impact in this world for the Kingdom of God. This information is intended to 1) clarify your own thinking on the subject, 2) present the fundamentals of spiritual warfare, and 3) stimulate your personal spiritual life toward a vibrant and dynamic relationship with God.

This book may even help you deal with your own personal problems that are caused by the enemy. A thorough reading of this book, coupled with further personal study, will help prepare you for ministering to others in this critical area. After reading a book like this, we cannot help but gain a new concern for those under the bondage and imprisonment of Satan.

ONE
SATAN'S PREDICAMENT

We must not be fooled into giving more credit to Satan than he deserves. He was cast out of heaven. He did not dethrone God. The Cross did seal Satan's doom. Even though Satan and his cohorts have power to operate in our world, they do not have unlimited power. God has set limits on what demons can and cannot do. If they could do whatever tickled their fancy, they would have reduced this world to shreds long ago.

An overview of the origin and fall of Satan will be valuable as a logical starting point and foundation for the chapters to come. Although the Bible does not describe his fall in precise and detailed terms, Scripture does provide foundational clues for an educated understanding of what occurred.

What exactly did Jesus mean by His statement in Luke 10:18, "I was watching Satan fall from heaven like lightening?" Was this a quasi-historical statement? In other words, did Jesus mean that in some great cosmic battle in ancient times, He actually saw Satan fall from heaven?

Perhaps Jesus was using a prophetic past tense often used in Hebrew, where an event which will assuredly occur in the future is spoken of as if it had already taken place. As the seventy returned with triumphant excitement from casting out demons, He saw in them, their message, their mission, and their authority, a vivid illustration of what the church would accomplish in the future.

Despite one's preferred interpretation of Luke 10:18, the *context* of this verse makes several things plain: first, Satan's home was in heaven with God; second, Satan fell from that radiant and joyful dwelling; third, there is a war in progress, and; fourth, God's people have power over the enemy.

Filling In the Missing Blanks

An examination of three additional passages helps to fill in some of the missing blanks concerning Satan's fall from heaven (Revelation 12, Ezekiel 26-28, Isaiah 14).

Revelation 12:7-9

> *And there was war in heaven, Michael and his angels waging war with the dragon. And the dragon and his angels waged war, and they were not strong enough, and there was no longer a place found for them in heaven. And the great dragon was thrown down, the serpent of old who is called the devil and Satan, who deceives the whole world; he was thrown down to the earth, and his angels were thrown down with him.*

These verses are found within what is commonly referred to as apocalyptic genre and must be treated with great care. They indicate that Satan had been an occupant of heaven, that he was one of the angelic spirits, and that he rebelled against God. Michael, the leader of the hosts of God, succeeds in casting the dragon out of heaven, along with one-third of the angels with him. As an expelled occupant of heaven, Earth is now the realm of Satan's operations.

Ezekiel also provides a glimpse of Satan's origin, as the doom of Tyre is prophesied in chapters 26-28. Tyre was an island kingdom lying northwest of Israel. Belonging to the Phoenicians, this land was without doubt one of the wealthiest kingdoms of its day and was filled with power and arrogance.

Verses 1-10 of chapter 28 speak of the prince of Tyre, while the next nine verses (11-17) speak of the king of Tyre. The language used of the prince of Tyre is appropriate to a man, for he is even called a man in verse nine. However, the language used of the king of Tyre seems to be highly inappropriate for any man.

It is interesting to note that the exact same spirit which dominates the king also dominates the prince. Both have tremendous beauty, wisdom, and power. Both defy God. The prince is the understudy of the king and is dominated by the spirit of the ultimate ruler of Tyre, Satan himself.

An examination and comparison of Ezekiel 28:1-10 and Ezekiel 28:11-17 reveal this point.

The King of Tyre Ezekiel 28:11-17

Again the word of the Lord came to me saying, "Son of Man, take up a lamentation over the king of Tyre, and say to him, 'Thus says the Lord God, "You had the seal of perfection, full of wisdom and perfect in beauty. You were in Eden, the garden of God; every precious stone was your covering: the ruby, the topaz, and the diamond; the beryl, the onyx, and the jasper; the lapis lazuli, the turquoise, and the emerald; and the gold, the workmanship of your settings and sockets, was in you. On the day you were created they were prepared. You were the anointed cherub who covers, and I placed you there. You were on the holy mountain of God; you walked in the midst of the stones of fire. You were blameless in your ways from the day you were created, until unrighteousness was found in you. By the abundance of your trade you were internally filled with violence, and you sinned; therefore I have cast you as profane from the mountain of God. And I have destroyed you, O covering cherub, from the midst of the stones of fire. Your heart was lifted up because of your beauty; you corrupted your wisdom by reason of your splendor. I cast you to the ground; I put you before kings, that they may see you."

The Prince of Tyre Ezekiel 28:1-10

The word of the Lord came again to me saying, "Son of man, say to the leader of Tyre, Thus says the Lord God, "Because your heart is lifted up and you have said, 'I am a god, I sit in the seat of gods, in the heart of the seas'; yet you are a man and not God, although you make your heart like the heart of God—behold, you are wiser than Daniel; there is no secret that is a match for you. By your wisdom and understanding you have acquired riches for yourself, and have acquired gold and silver for your treasuries. By your great wisdom, by your trade you have increased your riches, and your heart is lifted up because of your riches- Therefore, thus says the Lord God, 'Because you have made your heart like the heart of God, therefore, behold, I will bring strangers upon you, the most ruthless of the nations. And they will draw their swords against the beauty of your wisdom and defile your splendor. They will bring you down to the pit, and you will die the death of those who are slain in the heart of the seas. Will you still say, "I am a god," in the presence of your slayer, although you are a man and not God in the hands of those who wound you? You will die the death of the uncircumcised by the hand of strangers, for I have spoken!' declares the Lord God!"'"

Do you see any parallels between the two passages of Scripture? Although one refers to a man and the other to Satan, the spirit of the king, (i.e. Satan) dominates the prince. This prophecy reveals that Satan was a splendid and beautifully created cherub who once lived in heaven and enjoyed close intimacy with God. When sin was found in him, he was evicted from his heavenly abode. He did not leave quietly.

The final passage alluding to the origin and fall of Satan is found in Isaiah 14. Although there are differing rationales and understandings offered for the Ezekiel and Isaiah passages, it may be that a metaphorical hermeneutic applies best to both of these oracles. In other words, it may be appropriate to interpret these passages as metaphorically referring to Satan.

The context of Isaiah 14 finds the prophet taunting the king of Babylon. As with Ezekiel's prophecy, a more sinister figure lies behind the king of Babylon. Some of the verses in Isaiah 14, such as verses 12-14, could hardly apply to a man, but could easily apply to Satan, the king's master.

Isaiah 14:12-14

How you have fallen from heaven, O star of the morning, son of the dawn! You have been cut down to the earth, you who have weakened the nations! But you said in your heart, 'I will ascend to heaven; I will raise my throne above the stars of God, and I will sit on the mount of assembly in the recesses of the north. I will ascend above the heights of the clouds; I will make myself like the Most High.'

Satan was created with magnificent splendor and beauty after the order of the cherub. His rebellion against God led to a heavenly battle. He lost the challenge and was cast out of heaven, along with one-third of the angels.

Names and Activity of Satan

The Bible contains various names and descriptions for Satan and his demons. The following lists familiarize us with these references in Scripture. Although the names are used interchangeably, they still refer to the same phenomenon or persons. For instance, "devil," "Satan," and "tempter," all refer to the same entity. These lists reveal that Satan is a malicious enemy who does not have our best interest at heart.

Names and References for Satan and Demons

Satan

Satan, which means slanderer (Mk. 4:15, Rev. 12:4)
Devil, which means accuser (Mt. 4:1; Rev. 12:9)
Beelzebub, which may mean dung god (Mt. 12:24)
Belial, which means evil, wickedness, or worthlessness (2 Cor. 6:15)
Serpent (Gn. 3; Job 26:13; Is. 27:1; Lk. 10:19; 2 Cor. 11:3; Rev. 12:9, 14; 20:1)
Dragon (Rev. 12:3)
Lion (2 Tim. 4:17; 1 Pet. 5:8)
Strong one (Mt. 12:29; Mk. 3:27)
Wicked one (Mt. 6:13; 1 Jn. 3:12)
Accuser (Rev. 12:10)
Tempter (1 Thess. 3:5)
Adversary (1 Pet. 5:8)
Enemy (Mt. 13:39; Lk. 10:19)
Destroyer (Rev. 9:11)
Prince of demons (Mt. 12:24)
Prince of this world (Jn. 12:31)

God of this world (2 Cor. 4:4)
Prince of the power of the air (Eph. 2:2)

Demons

Principalities or rulers (Eph. 6:12; Col. 1:16)
Authorities (Eph. 3:10; Col. 2:15)
Powers (Rom. 8:38; 1 Pet. 3:22)
Dominions (Eph. 1:21; Col. 1:16)
Thrones (Col. 1:16)
Lords (1 Cor. 8:5)
Angels (Mt. 25:41; 2 Cor. 12:7; Rev. 12:7)
Demons (Lk. 8:30; Mk. 5:12; 8:31)
Unclean spirits (Mk. 9:25)
Evil spirits (Lk. 7:21; 8:2)
Elements (Col. 2:8)
Satyrs (Lev. 17:7; 2 Chron. 11:15)

Actions and Behaviors of Satan and Demons

Lying (Jn. 8:44)
Murdering (Jn. 8:44)
Tempting (Mt. 4:1)
Buffeting (2 Cor. 12:7)
Hindering (1 Thess. 2:18)
Sifting (Lk. 22:31)
Accusing (Zech. 3:1; Rev. 12:10)
Causing disease (Lk. 13:16)
Deceiving (2 Cor. 11:3; Rev. 12:9)
Corrupting minds (2 Cor. 11:3)
Devouring (1 Pet. 5:8)
Snatching away the world (Mt. 13:19)
Testing faith (Job 1:6-12)
Blinding minds (2 Cor. 4:4)
Causing a natural disaster (Job 1:12ff)
Trying to separate believers from Christ's love (Rom. 8:38-39)
Fighting against good angels (Rev. 12:7; Dan. 10:13)
Spreading false teaching (1 Kin. 22:21-23; 1 Tim. 4:1)

Causing mental disorders (Lk. 8:26-35)
Enticing individuals into moral and sexual impurity (Lk. 4:33,36)
Oppressing people (1 Sam. 18:10)
Indwelling people and animals (Lk. 8:2; Mk. 5:8-14)
Being used by God to punish evil nations (Ps. 78:49)
Being used by God to bring judgment on individuals (Judg. 9:23; 1 Sam. 16:14)
Being especially active at the end of the age (Rev. 9:1-12)
Fleeing like a coward (Jam. 4:7)

Satan's Destiny Is Sealed

Rather than being spectators sitting on the bleachers, Satan and his demons are active participants in the cosmic struggle. The Bible assures us that his destiny has forever been settled at the Cross of Calvary. Since the death and resurrection of Jesus Christ sealed Satan's destiny forever, we should not be frightened by his activity. The following verses represent a mere sample of what Scripture says concerning his destiny.

John 12:31

Now judgment is upon the world; now the ruler of this world shall be cast out.

John 16:11

...the ruler of this world is judged.

John 19:30

It is finished.

Matthew 25:41

Then He will also say to those on His left, "depart from Me, accursed ones, into the eternal fire which has been prepared for the devil and his angels."

Revelation 20:10

> *And the devil who deceived them was thrown into the lake of fire and brimstone, where the beast and the false prophet are also; and they will be tormented day and night forever.*

The Cross was the final event that sealed the judgment of Satan. Christ disarmed the rulers and authorities and made a public display of them, according to Colossians 2:15, "When He had disarmed the rulers and authorities, He made a public display of them, having triumphed over them through Him."

Hebrews 2:14 states, "that through death He might render powerless him who had the power of death, that is, the devil." The Cross is the momentous event which sealed Satan's final doom.

A Bee Without A Stinger

Satan's predicament is similar to a bumble bee buzzing through the air. As Jesus grabs the bee with His hand, the stinger is lodged in his palm. Jesus then releases the bee which goes about buzzing noisily and scaring a great many people. The bee is really harmless because it no longer has a stinger. Jesus took the pain and sting of the bee in our place. Since no stinger remains, all the bee can do is buzz around hoping to produce fear in individuals who still believe he can sting them.

According to 2 Thessalonians 2:9-11, Satan will have one last fling, producing counterfeit miracles and powerful delusions, but it is the last gasp for breath from a dying man.

The Cross has rendered Satan powerless and sealed his doom into the lake of fire (Mt. 25:41; Rev. 20:10). The only power Satan has over the children of God is that which they allow him to have. For now, we live in an interim period between the accomplishment of Calvary which sealed his doom, and the final execution of that accomplishment, as described in Revelation 20. Until that time, we put up with his obnoxious growling and irritating buzzing.

We must not be fooled into giving more credit to Satan than he deserves. He *was* cast out of heaven. He *did not* dethrone God. The

Cross *did seal* Satan's doom. Even though the devil and his cohorts have power to operate in our world, they do not have *unlimited* power. God has set limits on what demons can and cannot do. If they could do whatever tickled their fancy, they would have reduced this world to shreds long ago.

Demons are like collared dogs whose leashes only extend so far. They can operate within the leash area knowing that God willingly restrains His sovereignty to the obedience and faith of His children. Outside of the leash area, God's absolute sovereignty is unrestrained, and Satan must secure His permission before directly assaulting believers, as seen in both the story of Job (Job 1:9-12; 2:1-6) and Satan's request to sift Peter as wheat (Lk. 22:31).

The Power of the Cross

As with any war, there are major turning points which influence the outcome. In retrospect, we know that the invasion of Normandy, known as "D-Day," was the turning point which secured the defeat of Axis powers. D-Day was the beginning of a massive assault on German-occupied France in which 160,000 British, American, and Canadian troops landed on the beaches of Nazi held Normandy. It was the largest amphibious landing in history.

With success in Italy and along the eastern front, this invasion split the German war effort and ushered in the end of WW II. The success of D-Day ensured that the outcome of the war was not in doubt. Now the Allied powers could overtake the enemy resistance. Without the success of D-Day there would have been no V-E Day, victory in Europe.

This illustrates a very unique aspect regarding the spiritual warfare we face. The final outcome is never in doubt. Even though Satan's final destiny is secure, spiritual warfare still involves spiritual guns, bombs, and casualties because we live in the interim period between the event which sealed his doom and the actual implementation of that judgment.

However, the decisive battle has already been fought and won. Our spiritual D-Day took place at the Cross of Calvary. This victory is at the heart of what Jesus meant when He cried out, "It is finished" in John 19:30. The truth of this victory is also clearly stated by Paul in Colossians 2:15. In a sense, His death and resurrection stripped away any insignia of rank the enemy was wearing.

From the perspective of eternity, there has never been a time when Satan was not under the control of God. But from the perspective of time, a significant event occurred at the Cross.

Prior to the Cross, the people of God functioned with types and shadows as noted in Colossians 2:16-17 and Hebrews 8:5, 10:1. However, since the incarnation, death, and resurrection of Jesus Christ, we no longer operate in shadows and types, but on the basis of historical fact. The Old Testament looked *forward* to the Cross, while the New Testament is *grounded* upon that momentous event.

Christians gloriously sing of the Cross because it was there that the enemy was defeated once for all. Hebrews 2:14-15 states:

> *Since then the children share in flesh and blood, He Himself likewise also partook of the same, that through death He might render powerless him who had the power of death, that is, the devil; and might deliver those who through fear of death were subject to slavery all their lives.*

The Bible clearly tells us in Matthew 25:41 that eternal fire has been prepared for the devil and his angels. Revelation 20:10 also informs us that at some point in the future, Satan will be thrown into this lake of fire. Revelation 12:12 reveals that Satan is filled with fury because he is fully aware of his defeated status and knows that his time is short.

The Cross is the primary basis for our exercise of power over the forces of evil. Everything is related to, founded upon, and anchored in, the victory and resurrection of Jesus Christ who said in Matthew 28:18-19:

> *All authority has been given to Me in heaven and on earth. Go therefore and make disciples of all the nations, baptizing them in the name of the Father and the Son and the Holy Spirit, teaching them to observe all that I commanded you;*

and lo, I am with you always, even to the end of the age.

This commission obligates us to enforce this victory in our daily life and ministry.

T W O

FOUNDATIONAL ISSUES

In reality, Satan is nothing but a failure! His rebellion in heaven failed. His temptation of Jesus failed. His ability to keep you in his evil kingdom failed. Each time you glorify God, he fails. His middle name is failure. The fact that he challenged God and attempts to disrupt our lives today reveals his deep seated jealousy.

Even a casual perusal of the Bible reveals an ongoing spiritual battle from the beginning of Genesis to the end of Revelation. The biblical record concerning the fall of humankind places great enmity between Satan and human beings, "And I will put enmity between you and the woman, and between your seed and her seed; He shall bruise you on the head, and you shall bruise him on the heel." (Gen. 3:15).

This enmity extends even further as Satan blinds the minds of unbelievers to the truth of the gospel as noted in 2 Corinthians 4:4:

> *And even if our gospel is veiled, it is veiled to those who are perishing, in whose case the god of this world has blinded the minds of the unbelieving, that they might not see the light of the gospel of the glory of Christ, who is the image of God.*

In a broad sense, spiritual warfare begins the moment we are born, as Satan blinds our minds and tries everything in his power to keep us from following the Lord.

In a narrow sense, we become his hated enemy at the moment of our conversion. At conversion, we became new creatures in Christ (2 Cor. 5:17), delivered from the domain of darkness to the Kingdom of Christ (Col. 1:13). As new creatures, we partake in the nature of God (2 Pet. 1:4) by having the Holy Spirit reside in our lives (Eph. 1:13-14).

In light of the fierce battle raging throughout the biblical record, and between human beings and Satan, one questions why Satan was cast out of heaven. What was the rebellion and unrighteousness found in him? As a magnificent cherub angel charged with guarding the throne of God, (Ez. 28:14,16; Ex. 25:19; Ps. 18:10; Heb. 9:5), what did he do that deserved expulsion from heaven?

Satan is Jealous of God

The essence of the hostility is rooted in pride and jealousy. Satan became jealous of God and His glory. Instead of guarding, protecting, and promoting God's glory, Satan desired to possess it all for himself. This is seen in two key New Testament passages (Mt. 4:8-10; 2 Thess. 2:4), as well as Isaiah 14 and Ezekiel 28, which have been previously mentioned.

During the wilderness experience of forty days and forty nights, the devil's personal ambition is clearly exposed in his final temptation of Jesus in Matthew 4:8-9:

> *Again, the devil took Him to a very high mountain, and showed Him all the kingdoms of the world, and their glory; and he said to Him, all these things will I give you, if you fall down and worship me.*

The temptations began with turning stones into bread, and moved on to a jump off the temple pinnacle. Lest we think Jesus was only tempted three times, the other gospels (Mk. 1; Lk. 4) indicate that He was tempted by the devil throughout His entire 40 days in the wilderness.

With mounting frustration, Satan's final wilderness temptation carelessly reveals his true desire, to be w like God is w! Satan gave it his best shot, but even his finest effort could not persuade Jesus to falter.

2 Thessalonians 2:4 supports this revealed motive of Satan. Speaking of the man of lawlessness, Paul states that he, "opposes and exalts himself above every so-called god or object of worship, so that he takes his seat in the temple of God, displaying himself as

being God." The man of lawlessness, the incarnation of Satan, has as his main goal to establish himself as God.

Satan's jealous motives and insatiable thirst to be like God is also vividly seen in Ezekiel 28 and Isaiah 14 quoted below.

Isaiah 14:12-14

> *How you have fallen from heaven, O star of the morning, son of the dawn! You have been cut down to the earth, you who have weakened the nations! But you said in your heart, 'I will ascend to heaven; I will raise my throne above the stars of God, and I will sit on the mount of assembly in the recesses of the north. I will ascend above the heights of the clouds; I will make myself like the Most High.'*

The Five "I Wills" of Satan

The five "I wills" of Satan found in these verses further illuminate his true inner desires, since they are said to come from his heart. Satan first said, "I will ascend to heaven." Dissatisfied with his status as a created being, his unholy ambition yearns to enter a realm of being reserved exclusively for God. Instead of bending his knee in humble adoration to the only true and living God, the repulsive desire of Satan is that others, including God Himself, would actually worship him.

Secondly, Satan has said in his heart, "I will raise my throne above the stars of God." Since Daniel 8:9-10 and Revelation 12:4 refer to angels as stars, it is easy to discern Satan's discontentment with his angelic status. In his jealous desire for authority, he aspires to be over and above all the other angels.

The third boast which pours from his innermost being is, "I will sit on the mount of assembly." If the "mount of assembly" is the center of God's earthly rule and refers to the throne of the Messiah, as many scholars believe, then Satan is challenging Christ's role as authoritative king. In his wilderness temptation quest, Satan utterly failed to usurp Christ's authoritative role, yet he boldly desires to claim the power and position which belongs to Christ alone.

His fourth claim declares, "I will ascend above the heights of the clouds." In the Old Testament, it is not unusual for clouds to be associated with God's glory as seen in Exodus 13:21, 40:34-38, and 1 Kings 8:10-11:

Exodus 13:21

And the Lord was going before them in a pillar of cloud by day to lead them on the way, and in a pillar of fire by night to give them light, that they might travel by day and by night.

Exodus 40:34-38

Then the cloud covered the tent of meeting, and the glory of the Lord filled the tabernacle. And Moses was not able to enter the tent of meeting because the cloud had settled on it, and the glory of the Lord filled the tabernacle. And throughout all their journeys whenever the cloud was taken up from over the tabernacle, the sons of Israel would set out; but if the cloud was not taken up, then they did not set out until the day when it was taken up. For throughout all their journeys, the cloud of the Lord was on the tabernacle by day, and there was fire in it by night, in the sight of all the house of Israel.

1 Kings 8:10-11

And it came about when the priests came from the holy place, that the cloud filled the house of the Lord, so that the priests could not stand to minister because of the cloud, for the glory of the Lord filled the house of the Lord.

Satan craves the glorious position solely occupied by our Heavenly Father. Instead of *reflecting* God's glory, he wants it all for himself.

Finally, the fifth and last "I will" spewing forth from the inner chambers of Satan's heart declares, "I will make myself like the Most High." This is his ultimate objective. He defies and confronts the sovereign position of the one true God, Yahweh. But the created one can never rise to the position of the Creator.

The drive to reach one's goals at any cost blurs even the sharpest vision. Satan's selective perception conveniently overlooks biblical passages which affirm that there is no one like God:

Isaiah 43:10b

Before me there was no God formed and there will be none after me.

Isaiah 44:6

Thus says the Lord, the King of Israel and his Redeemer, the Lord of hosts: 'I am the first and I am the last, and there is no God besides Me.'

Isaiah 45:5-6

I am the Lord, and there is no other; besides me there is no God. I will gird you, though you have not known Me; that men may know from the rising to the setting of the sun that there is no one besides Me. I am the Lord, and there is no other.

Isaiah 45:21-23

Declare and set forth your case; indeed, let them consult together. Who has announced this from of old? Who has long since declared it? Is it not I, the Lord? And there is no other God besides Me, a righteous God and Savior; there is none except Me. Turn to Me, and be saved, all the ends of the earth; for I am God, and there is no other. I have sworn by Myself, the word has gone forth from My mouth in righteousness and will not turn back, that to Me every knee will bow, every tongue will swear allegiance.

Satan is Jealous of Believers

Although the conflict is deeply entrenched in pride, another interesting twist to the "jealousy factor" enters into the picture.

Satan is not only jealous of God, he is also jealous of human beings created in the "image of God."

There are two main reasons for Satan's jealous outlook toward the followers of Christ. First, all humans were created in God's image. Second, while created lower than the angels for our time on earth, we were also created with the potential for glorification. We have the capacity for a likeness to God which Satan will never attain. Indeed, several verses of Scripture, such as Romans 8:17,30 and 9:23, speak of the wonderful glorification believers will experience as part of God's plan:

Romans 8:17,30

> *17 ...we suffer with Him in order that we may also be glorified with Him.*
>
> *30 and whom He predestined, these He also called; and whom He called, these He also justified; and whom He justified, these He also glorified.*

Romans 9:23

> *And He did so in order that He might make known the riches of His glory upon vessels of mercy, which He prepared beforehand for glory.*

Even though Satan was created as a magnificent cherub, as an angel, he can never claim to have been created in the image of God. According to Genesis 1:26-27, that privilege is strictly reserved for human beings. Since glory lies at the core of his rebellious motives, it is not surprising to discover that he is also jealous of believers who will one day be glorified into a state which he can never attain.

It cannot be stated strongly enough, that the central issue of spiritual warfare is the glory of God. Satan desires what he can never possess. While pursuing a hopeless dream, he will do everything in his power to disrupt the flow of glory to God.

As a cherub angel, he led a rebellion against God which failed miserably and resulted in his expulsion from heaven. That he even tried a frontal attack seems absurd when one considers the vast difference between the Creator and the created one. Satan does not even come close to being on the same level as God. Usurping God's glorious position was an impossibility. The challenge was absolutely ludicrous!

In reality, Satan is nothing but a failure! His rebellion in heaven failed. His temptation of Jesus failed. His ability to keep you in his evil kingdom failed. Each time you glorify God, he fails. His middle name is failure. The fact that he challenged God and attempts to disrupt our lives today reveals his deep seated jealousy.

Stealing Glory Away From God

Realizing the futility of a direct attack against God, Satan assaults believers in an attempt to *indirectly* harm God. Like a spoiled brat, if he cannot possess the glory which belongs only to God, he will attempt to rob believers of their ability to bestow glory upon their Heavenly Father.

In the realm of everyday living, this glory issue might be played out in the sample scenario of Karen, a cashier who works in a local department store. She notices how easy it would be to take a few bills here and there while ringing up customers.

If she succumbs to the temptation and pockets the money, the glory which ascends to God through obedience is now lost. However, the devil loses if she says, "No way Satan, stealing is not right!" This simple situation either brings glory to God or robs Him of potential glory that could have been attributed to Him. Righteous behavior undermines Satan's goals and brings glory to God.

Since Satan cannot overtake God directly, he attacks His children in an effort to steal away glory from God. It is the way of a coward, but he is at times effective, especially upon those who are unaware of the relationship between glory and spiritual warfare.

We know how jealousy operates. Jealousy not only desires what the other person possesses, but it may even hate the other person for having it. Jealous behavior tries to deprive others from having what we cannot possess. It is childish, but Satan does this by attacking the children of God.

Although we have been created in God's image, the glory we are able to bestow upon our Lord directly stems from a vibrant, dynamic, and ongoing relationship with Him. Satan longs to fracture that relationship. The power of jealous envy is the energy and motivation that sustains his efforts against us.

Satan is nothing more than a jealous fallen angel who desires to be a god and receive the glory which belongs to God alone. Since his full frontal assault was unsuccessful, he instigates guerrilla warfare upon God's children, inducing them to stumble, fall, and ultimately deprive God of the glory brought about through obedience.

The Influence of Perception

One's perception on any given issue will color, or bias, the way that issue is viewed. A vivid reminder of this fact occurs as I reminisce about my wife's grandmother. During my days in seminary, we often made the half hour drive across the river for a delightful visit. Grandma's home was a botanist's delight. Rarely would we leave without taking home one of her repotted plants.

Knowing how much she loved to garden and feed hungry birds during the winter, one of the relatives bought her a bag of potting soil and birdseed as a Christmas gift. This gift weighed heavy on her mind, for it was all she talked about.

Looking for us to confirm her worst fears, she repeatedly said, "Can you believe it? They gave me a sack of dirt for Christmas. How rude!" Unfortunately, she misread this Christmas event. What was intended to be a loving gift was interpreted as a discourteous act. Her totally inaccurate assessment was based upon a negative and faulty perception of the gift.

In a similar way, the problem of perception, or the problem of worldview as it is often referred to, also occurs in spiritual warfare. In the United States, our worldview often makes it far easier to believe in the theological, or theoretical aspect of spiritual warfare than it does to incorporate that theology into our everyday life.

In other words, where the rubber meets the road in the practical realm, Satan, spirits, and demons, are not very real to many of us.

They belong in a seminary classroom, a theological textbook, or an amazing missionary story nestled in a strange and remote land.

For example, we are usually more aware of the people who live *around* us, than we are of the Holy Spirit who lives *within* us. Our awareness of, and sensitivity to, spiritual warfare is greatly influenced by our perception of demons, spirits, and Satan. How can we successfully overcome the enemy when we confine him to a seminary textbook, or to a theological discussion? But when we perceive Satan as a viable adversary, engaged in a war against the followers of Christ, we develop a heightened sensitivity to his schemes of deception.

Deficient Worldviews

A worldview is defined as:

> *the thought system we develop for explaining the world around us and our experiences in it. It is determined almost entirely by the society in which we grow up. In most instances, it is something we absorb subconsciously more than something we adopt after careful study..."*[3]

In short, our presuppositions and assumptions color our understanding of reality.

In order to comprehend and interpret the events which occur around us, we tend to divide and classify circumstances according to our view of how life functions and operates. However, a true and accurate assessment of our experiences is predicated upon an accurate classification system. If our understanding does not perceive the reality of Satan's opposition, we will wrongly classify the experience. If our worldview is inaccurate, our interpretation of our world will also be inaccurate. A proper perspective is essential for successful Christian living.

Our worldview is always communicated more by what we *do* than what we *say*. Actions speak louder than words. The husband who says to his wife, "I love you," but acts otherwise, reveals his true feelings toward her. Those who publicly declare the importance of church attendance and never attend church, reveal their true outlook on the issue. If people say how much they depend on God, the truth of their profession will be seen in a crisis situation. This is when faith and trust are most accurately measured.

People will always live according to what they *believe*, but not always according to what they *profess*. Worldview is what people believe, and what people believe is revealed by what they *do* more than what they *say*. If our worldview includes a healthy understanding of the reality of spiritual warfare, we will be better prepared to stand against the enemy.

Worldview Illustrated

A helpful illustration of worldview is seen in the wearing of three pairs of eyeglasses, one in front of the other. It is easy to imagine wearing one pair of glasses, because people do this every day. For the sake of our illustration, imagine someone actually wearing three different pair of glasses, each stacked in front of one another.

The rays of light from the sun, which represent true reality, must travel through three pairs of lenses in order to reach our eyes. The first pair of glasses are called "conceivable lenses." They represent what we believe is possible, attainable, and conceivable. If we do not believe spiritual warfare is possible, then we downplay its reality and mistake its impact.

The second pair of glasses are called "experience lenses" and represent the experiences, events, and circumstances we have encountered during our journey through life. We tend to evaluate our present situation through our past experiences.

The third pair of glasses contain "analysis lenses" which help us analyze, scrutinize, and interpret the light rays. Our analysis of what is real is based on what we believe is possible and what we have experienced in the past.

In essence, our perception of reality comes only after it is filtered through the lenses of what we conceive is possible, what we have personally experienced, and what we analyze, or interpret, those experiences to mean.

Three Main Worldviews

Three main worldviews regarding God, demons, and spiritual power exist among the people of today's world: the animistic worldview, the scientific worldview, and the scriptural worldview.

Animistic Worldview

Although this belief system is not prevalent among our culture, it does exist to a large extent outside of the Western regions. Animism believes that spiritual power permeates everything in the world. Thus, this same spiritual power can be in a rock, a cow, or a plant. It is capable of permeating anything and everything.

For animists, spiritual power is a neutral force to be manipulated for good or evil. Just as nuclear energy can provide power to the homes of thousands of people, it can also be fashioned into a bomb with the intent to kill and destroy life.

To imagine a world where spirit beings are separate and distinct from life itself is inconceivable to animists. In their worldview, the natural and supernatural realms are so intricately linked together that they are forever mixed and inseparable.

Scientific Worldview

The scientific worldview, on the other hand, is the standard persuasion of the Western world. This view, with its compulsion for logic and precision, has divided reality into two distinct parts, the supernatural and the natural spheres. Everything is placed in an "either-or" category. It is either religious or secular, spiritual or physical, sacred or secular, material or immaterial, psychological or spiritual, faith or fact, demonic or physical, etc.

The scientific worldview has created two separate and distinct compartments which do not interact with one another. God lives in the heavenlies and humans live on this planet. God may have established natural laws to govern the physical universe, but now there is no need for Him to interact at all.

When something occurs in the physical world it has a logical, natural cause that can be scientifically explained and validated. It is extremely rare for spirit beings living in the supernatural domain to influence or interact with humans living in a natural, physical place. Although miracles do happen, God sits on His heavenly throne overseeing the care of heavenly functions, while His established scientific laws operate the Earth below. God and angels stay put in the supernatural realm.

Some individuals feel this view is "Christian" because it advocates a supernatural realm and holds that God is the Creator. The problem, however, is that the two separate compartments into which they categorize reality never interact with one another. From a scientific viewpoint, spiritual warfare is a balloon without air. If Satan and evil spirits do not interact with humans on the Earth, then what exactly is the point and definition of spiritual warfare? If the spiritual domain does not connect with the physical world, then spiritual warfare is an abstract concept, not a practical reality.

Animistic and scientific worldviews play right into the hand of Satan. Both of these outlooks are deficient in their assessment of the world around them. The animists never separate the spiritual from the physical, while the scientific assessment rarely, if ever, allows them to interact.

Scriptural Worldview

A scriptural worldview brings with it the balance needed to correctly interpret the world around us and accurately assess the status of our foe. This outlook maintains that there are three different beings interacting together: God, angels, and humans.

Scripture supports the concept of a spiritual realm and a physical realm. However, the two are connected by the presence, function, and activities of both good and evil angels.

There are many angels and there are many human beings, but there is only one God. He is eternal and has always existed. No one created Him. He knows all things and maintains all power and control. He is one of a kind. There is no other like Him. Satan possesses none of these attributes and neither do we. This is a place reserved only for the holy of holies, God Himself. No one even comes close to claiming the role and place of God.

Human beings dwell on Earth. We are confined to temporal bodies living in a physical world, put here by God to bring glory to His name (Ps. 19; Eph. 1:6,12). Paul instructs us in 1 Corinthians 10:31 to give glory to God in all that we do, "Whether, then, you eat or drink or whatever you do, do all to the glory of God."

Since we were created to bring God glory, and spiritual warfare revolves around the issue of glory, Satan rages a furious battle to prevent us from accomplishing our task. If he can deceive us into maintaining a faulty worldview regarding his activities on Earth, then his dirty work goes unrestrained. The spiritual warfare this book is concerned with takes place on Earth as evil spirits interact with human beings.

Angels, on the other hand, move between Earth and the heavenlies. Since angels are created beings (Col. 1:16), they cannot in any way claim to be on the same level as God.

Scripture contains over three hundred references to angels. Although we do not know exactly how many of them exist, they must be large in number as seen in such verses as Psalm 68:17, Daniel 7:10, and Hebrews 12:22.

Angels interact in various ways with our world. God uses them to carry out His plans and minister to His children. The following list details several activities in which angels may be involved:

Activities of Angels

Angels praise and worship God. (Ps.103:20; 148; Rev. 7:11-12)

Angels may provide protection from danger. (2 Kin. 6:17)

Angels may provide guidance. (Gen. 22:11-12,15-18; 24:7; 31:11-12; Dan. 8:15-16; 9:20-22; 10:12-13; Mt. 1:20)

Angels may provide deliverance from an enemy. (Gen. 19; Dan. 3:19-28; Acts 5:19-20; 12:6-11)

Angels may destroy enemies. (Gen. 19:13; 2 Chron. 32:21;

Ps. 78:49; Is. 37:36; Acts 12:23)

Angels may provide food. (1 Kin. 19:4-8)

Angels provide acts of ministry to believers. (Heb. 1:14)

Angels may interact with nature. (2 Sam. 24:15-16; Ex. 14:19; Num. 20:16; Mt. 28:2; Rev. 7:1-2; 16)

God, angels, and human beings are separate and distinct from one another, yet they all interact together. God's involvement with this world entails the use of angels to accomplish His plans.

The ugly side of this interaction is the realization that when Satan fell from heaven, he took with him one-third of the angels (Rev. 12:4). Since they were unable to dethrone God, they live out the rest of their existence alienated from Him, always attempting to disrupt, as much as possible, the lives of His children.

The scientific view to which much of the Western world adheres, eliminates any belief in the activity of angels with this physical world. Because this worldview is unbiblical and unbalanced, so is the understanding and awareness of spiritual warfare for its adherents.

Facts are not changed by one's belief, or lack of belief. The atheist may deny the existence of God, but that does not mean God does not exist. In like manner, just because people do not believe Satan and demons are involved in their lives, does not make it true. The only accurate worldview is one that is solidly anchored to Scripture.

Our perception of reality, our worldview, either helps us in our battle against Satan, or contributes to his deceptive strategies in our lives. Many Christians have unwittingly succumbed to a scientific worldview which boasts of a biblical foundation, but in reality eliminates God's involvement in this world through angels.

Three

DEMON POSSESSION

Satan and demons own nothing. They prowl around this world with puffed up chests believing it all belongs to them. Although this may be their stomping grounds, they are only here by the permission of God, not by any inherent right of their own. As their Creator and Judge, God actually owns them. They are nothing more than intruders vociferously attempting to claim territory that does not rightfully belong to them.

It has been said by many on more than one occasion, "I do not believe Christians can be possessed by the devil, so I do not want to get involved in a study which goes against my understanding of Scripture."

This type of response is disturbing for two reasons. First, it is often nothing more than a religious and euphemistic way of hiding fear. Fear and misunderstanding conjure up weird images of people slithering on the floor, or sensational films such as "The Exorcist." Because of fear, some individuals would rather remain in a comfortable ignorance than learn the truth.

Second, a mind at rest tends to stay at rest. Maintaining a growing and learning posture is expected of Christ's followers. We are encouraged, in 2 Peter 1:5-7, to add knowledge and other qualities to our faith. 2 Peter 1:9-10 declares that if we do not continually add to our faith, we become short-sighted:

> *For if these qualities are yours and are increasing, they render you neither useless nor unfruitful in the true knowledge of our Lord Jesus Christ. For he who lacks these qualities is blind or short-sighted, having forgotten his purification from his former sins.*

The study of spiritual warfare is not intended to scare people. Its purpose is to challenge and clarify our understanding of the subject and help us stand strong and victorious over the enemy.

Dismissing any discussion of demon possession in fear that it might upset our already established, safe, and comfortable viewpoint, goes against the attitude of new learning advocated by Peter. Putting our mind in neutral and shoving our head in the sand leads to spiritual short-sightedness. Terms such as "demon possession" demand further thinking and clarification.

Definition of Terms

When asked if Christians can be demon possessed, I usually respond by asking the inquirer to define the term which has caused so much confusion. If everyone were on the same definitional playing field, there would be a lot more agreement and a lot less bewilderment. The phrase "demon possession" and "demon possessed" are unfortunate and inaccurate terms chosen by Bible translators to convey the meaning of the original Greek.

Our English word "demon" comes from the Greek noun "daimon." This is a good transliteration. However, the Greek verb "daimonizomai" has been translated "demon possessed" when a more accurate transliteration is "demonized."

Demon possession confines us to an "either/or" mode as someone is either demon possessed or not demon possessed. Using the correct phrase "demonized" allows us to move beyond two limited categories and speak of the extent or degree one is influenced by Satan. When accurately translated as "demonized," our understanding of the phrase more precisely reflects the Scriptural expression.

The Issue of Ownership

Also muddying the water is the term "possession," which implies the notion of ownership. I possess a car, a home, a baseball glove, a camera, a computer, and many other things. They are mine. I own them. However, to think of Satan and demons "owning" Christians is clearly unthinkable in light of Scripture.

Colossians 1:13 states, "For He delivered us from the domain of darkness, and transferred us to the kingdom of His beloved Son."

Also affirming our relationship with God, 1 John 3:1 states:

> *See how great a love the Father has bestowed upon us, that we should be called children of God; and such we are. For this reason the world does not know us, because it did not know Him.*

We are spiritually begotten by God the Father. We are His workmanship (Eph. 2:10) and partake of His divine nature (2 Pet. 1:4) through the resident Holy Spirit given to us as a down payment of our future blessing (Eph. 1:13-14). Numerous passages could be cited conveying the truth that Christians belong to God.

Satan and demons own nothing. They prowl around this world with puffed up chests believing it all belongs to them. Although this may be their stomping grounds, they are only here by the permission of God, not by any inherent right of their own. As their Creator and Judge, God actually owns them. They are nothing more than intruders vociferously attempting to claim territory that does not rightfully belong to them.

Satan wants us to think that he is powerful and manipulative to the point where our involvement in spiritual warfare surely means our defeat. He wants us to believe that we should stay away from him, rather than pursue the truth about him.

The horrifying image we have created of Satan and demons can now be laid to rest. In the darkness of my room as a young child, I distinctly remember seeing a large gorilla in my closet. In the morning light, however, I realized the frightening image I created in my mind was nothing more than clothes on hangers. A correct understanding of the term "demon possession" deflates old frightening myths about the evil one.

The Cartwright Illustration

Though Christians cannot be *owned* by Satan, he can *influence* or *control* certain aspects of their life. The rolling acreage from the once popular television show entitled "Bonanza" may be a useful illustration for understanding this concept. As you recall, Ben Cartwright owned an enormous amount of property. The Cartwright bonanza could easily be seen on the map which burst into flames during the television introduction.

Inevitably, intruders would trespass on the Cartwright land while Little Joe, Adam, and Hoss drove them off the property, repaired damaged fences, and asserted their authority over the Cartwright estate.

Imagine that our life is represented by all of the acreage involved in the Cartwright ranch. The large Cartwright home represents the core of our identity as a child of God. It is the place where the Holy Spirit dwells. Within the boundaries of the Cartwright ranch are all the specific areas of our life. Our thought life lies to the West. The financial aspect of our life lies to the East, and so on.

As much as Satan would like, he cannot overthrow or conquer the large Cartwright home. That is where the Holy Spirit lives and Satan cannot own what the Holy Spirit owns. Since he is unable to conquer our home, he crosses barbed wire perimeter fences to invade and attack the outlying areas. In other words, if he cannot own us, he attempts to disrupt the various areas of our life which have the potential for bringing honor and glory to God.

Just as Little Joe, Adam, and Hoss asserted the Cartwright name, kicked off the intruders, and repaired any damage, Christians must do likewise. Like a guerrilla force, Satan breaks through the borders of our life producing small pockets of armed resistance. He will remain within the border causing as much destruction as possible unless we assert our identity and authority as a child of God, drive him off the property, repair any damage inflicted, and prepare ourselves for his next deceptive attack.

The issue at stake for the believer is not one of ownership, but one of control and influence. This is why Paul urged believers in Ephesians 5:18 to allow the Holy Spirit control of their lives, "And do not get drunk with wine, for that is dissipation, but be filled with the Spirit." The controlling influence for a follower of Christ is to be the Holy Spirit of God.

Paul further writes in Romans 12:1, that we are to present our bodies as a living and holy sacrifice to God:

I urge you therefore, brethren, by the mercies of God, to present your bodies a living and holy sacrifice, acceptable to God, which is your spiritual service of worship.

In Romans 6:13 he also states:

Do not go on presenting the members of your body to sin as instruments of unrighteousness; but present yourselves to God as those alive from the dead, and your members as instruments of righteousness to God.

Christians belong to God both by creation and by redemption. We were created by God as seen in Psalm 100:3, "Know that the Lord Himself is God; it is He who has made us, and not we ourselves; we are His people and the sheep of His pasture."

We also belong to God because of redemption, as seen in 1 Corinthians 6:19-20:

Or do you not know that your body is a temple of the Holy Spirit who is in you, whom you have from God, and that you are not your own? For you have been bought with a price: therefore glorify God in your body.

These, and other verses, clearly reveal that the only control and influence to which believers should yield themselves, is that of the Holy Spirit. To be controlled or influenced by someone or something other than God is not in keeping with Scripture.

Levels of Demonization

Often, writers on this subject present various levels of demonic influence that can occur in the life of a believer such as subjection, oppression, obsession, and actual indwelling of the body by an evil spirit. Although these terms may vary, they are attempts to label differing degrees of demonic influence.

We know that demons afflict some more than others, but a classification which attempts to differentiate the degrees of affliction has no solid biblical basis. The Bible does not offer an ordered set of labels for varying degrees of influence. Any such influence, whether mild or severe in our eyes, is still the result of demons invading territory that does not rightfully belong to them, and steps must be taken to put them back in their rightful place.

Is Demonic Influence Real?

It is difficult for many to make the distinction between ownership and influence. They dismiss spiritual warfare or "demonization" because they automatically equate the term "demon possession" with ownership. The question is not whether Christians can be owned by Satan, for the answer is clearly no, but it is possible for believers to experience demonic influence and control with certain aspects of their lives.

What follows is a brief interaction with several arguments put forth by those who do not support the notion of satanic and demonic influence in the life of a believer. Fred Dickason, in his work entitled *Demon Possession and the Christian*, more fully addresses each of these arguments.[4]

Good and Evil Together?

Some believe that the Holy Spirit and an evil spirit cannot be in the same body at the same time. Since the body of a Christian is the temple of the Holy Spirit, demons cannot be where the Spirit is. Scriptures such as 1 Corinthians 2:12; 6:9-20; 2 Corinthians 6:14-18; James 3:12; and 1 John 4:4 are used to support this view. However, none of these passages state that a demon cannot enter into a Christian. The argument is based on human logic, which is frail at best, and not the teaching of Scripture.

From one of my college courses entitled "Introduction to Logic," we were taught that conclusions are only as good as the premises they are built upon. Opponents logically conclude that since all Christians are indwelt by the Holy Spirit and demons cannot dwell where the Spirit is, then Christians cannot have demons.

It is true that all believers are indwelt by the Holy Spirit, but it is not true that demons and the Holy Spirit cannot be in the same place at the same time. Thus, the conclusion that Christians cannot have demons is based on a faulty assumption.

The danger of a faulty premise might be more easily seen in the following example. All chickens have feathers. All pillows have feathers. Therefore, all pillows are chickens. Obviously, since the second premise is false, the conclusion is suspect.

This view is not only problematic because it lacks proper Scriptural support, but also because we find Satan directly entering into the presence of God in the book of Job (1:6-12; 2:1-7). How can this be if God and evil cannot be in the same place at the same time? If this ill-fated argument were extended to its logical conclusion, God's omnipresence would preclude demons from being anywhere. Since God is everywhere present, where in the world could demons go to escape from the presence of God?

The possibility of receiving "another spirit," one which is obviously different than the Holy Spirit, is given as a warning to believers in 2 Corinthians 11:4. In Ephesians 4:27, Paul also warns against giving Satan a foothold in our life. The word "foothold" in the original Greek language is the word "topos," from which we acquire the English word "topography." It refers to a place, region, or locality and is used over 80 times in Scripture. The obvious place where individuals could give Satan a foothold, is in their own lives.

Additionally, numerous Scriptural passages speak of Satan's activity and his ability to control and influence people (Mt. 7:13-29; 2 Cor. 11:3-4, 13-15; 2 Thess. 2:1-17; 1 Tim. 1:19-20; 3:6-7; 4; 5:9-15; 2 Tim. 2:14-26; 1 Jn. 4:1-4; Rev. 13).

The Corinthian and James passages state that a mixture of good and evil should not be in the same person, but acknowledges that, in fact, it can be. The argument that evil and good cannot be in the same place at the same time falls far short of the kind of support needed to sustain it.

God Automatically Protects Believers

Another "so-called" proof offered against demonic activity in the life of the believer is the idea that God *automatically* protects

His children, therefore demons cannot invade what God protects. Passages such as 1 John 3:8; 5:18, Romans 8:35-39, Colossians 1:12-13, and Ephesians 2:1-2 are often used for support.

However, one does not have to read the Bible for long before discovering that protection is not automatic. Ephesians 6:10-18, James 4:7, 1 Peter 5:8-9, 2 Corinthians 2:11, and 1 John 4:1-6 all speak clearly of the need for believers to be self-controlled and alert in order to resist the enemy. 1 Peter 5:8-9 says:

> *Be of sober spirit, be on the alert. Your adversary, the devil, prowls about like a roaring lion, seeking someone to devour. But resist him, firm in your faith, knowing that the same experiences of suffering are being accomplished by your brethren who are in the world.*

In a similar vein, why would God, in Ephesians 6, lay armor at our feet, command us to put it on and utilize it if we already had His automatic protection? If direct Satanic opposition is possible for Christians, a false perception of God's automatic protection will leave us as vulnerable victims of Satan's ruthless attacks. The protection of God is maintained through obedience, holy living, and the utilization of the protective armor He provides for us.

Our Enemy is External, Not Internal

Others believe that the armor of God is for an external enemy, not an internal one. This is true, but the whole object of the armor is to keep the enemy out. If there is no real chance of the enemy's flaming arrows penetrating our life, there is no real reason to utilize the armor. The entire purpose of the armor is to keep an external enemy, an external enemy.

It is often stressed that the struggle Christians face internally is between the spirit and the flesh, not between the spirit and demons. However, many Scriptural passages indicate that the flesh, the world, and demons work together. An inability to control the flesh can be an open doorway for demonic activity. This is why Paul implores us to yield the members of our bodies for good instead of evil, to God instead of the devil. The possibility of demonic strongholds in our life is abruptly diminished when we yield ourselves to the Holy Spirit.

Demon Talk is Taboo

Finally, many believe that talk of demonic activity actually does more harm than good. Informing someone that they may be experiencing demonic influence only complicates the original problem. Actually, quite the opposite is true. To reveal Satan's clandestine operation and discover effective methods for defeating him leads to victorious Christian living and greater levels of confidence in Christ. Freedom from demonic bondage is life-giving. Withholding pertinent information for fear of upsetting counselees does absolutely nothing to relieve their problem.

It is impossible for Satan to *own* Christians, but it is possible for Christians to experience his attacks and influence to varying degrees. If the provisions of God are not utilized, Satan may gain a stronghold in our life and through that stronghold, exercise control and influence over a particular issue or issues.

A demon can never indwell a believer in the same sense as the Holy Spirit. According to John 14:6, the Holy Spirit enters a believer at the moment of conversion and is a permanent guest, never to leave, "And I will ask the Father, and He will give you another Helper, that He may be with you forever."

Demons, on the other hand, invade territory that is not their own and can be evicted. They cannot rightfully or permanently indwell a believer as the Holy Spirit does, and they can never exercise control in any area in which the Holy Spirit is in control.

Causes of Demonic Activity

Satan does not spin the wheel of chance to determine who he attacks. There are specific behaviors which may lead to a demonic stronghold in one's life. If we play with fire we may get burned.

Personal sin, involvement in the occult, and ancestral sin are major entry points for demonic activity and should remind us to remove ourselves from anything that might provide fuel for his fire.

Personal Sin

There are two categories of personal sin, past and present. Past sins are those which were committed in the past but have never adequately been confessed, forsaken, and cleansed, such as an association with the occult, or a past problem with pornography.

Present sins are those which are current and active in our lives, such as pride, bitterness, and anger.

Satan can gain access to our lives through the open door of sin. He is not there because of any inherent right of his own, he simply takes advantage of the access we provide him.

The key to removing this stronghold is confession. When believers sin, the Spirit of God works to convict them of that sin. If they respond to that conviction with confession, they receive cleansing as promised in 1 John 1:9, "If we confess our sins, He is faithful and righteous to forgive us our sins and to cleanse us from all unrighteousness."

As a consequence of personal sin, King Saul was attacked by a spirit in 1 Samuel 16:16. A lack of repentance for his disobedience made him a prime target for an enemy assault. Similarly, deceitfulness and willful lying were at play with Ananias and Sapphira who died for their sins in Acts 5:1-11.

2 Corinthians 2:10-11 makes it clear that Satan will take advantage of the unforgiveness within us if we do not properly confess our sin:

> *But whom you forgive anything, I forgive also; for indeed what I have forgiven, if I have forgiven anything, I did it for your sakes in the presence of Christ, in order that no advantage be taken of us by Satan; for we are not ignorant of his schemes.*

Because of boasting and immorality, Paul urged that such individuals be turned over to Satan for the destruction of their flesh in 1 Corinthians 5:1-7. In Galatians 3:1, Paul describes the Galatians as having been "bewitched" by believing false teaching. Although they should have recognized the false teaching of the Judaizers, they were mislead. This provided Satan with the tactical advantage.

Ephesians 4:26-27 declares that anger, not dealt with in a timely matter, may provide the devil with an opportunity, "Be angry, and yet do not sin; do not let the sun go down on your anger, and do not give the devil an opportunity." In 1 Timothy 1:19-20 Paul delivered Hymenaeus and Alexander over to Satan because they rejected their faith. 1 Timothy 3:6-7 warns new believers against pride lest they fall into the snare of the devil. James 3:13-16 clearly cautions against bitter jealousy and selfish ambition which is demonic and leads to disorder. Paul admonishes the Corinthian believers, in 2 Corinthians 11:3, to beware of false teaching which Satan uses to deceive, just as he deceived Eve.

Overwhelming Scriptural evidence reveals that sin opens a door for Satan to gain a stronghold in our lives. Obviously, one way to avoid demonic strongholds is to walk a righteousness path.

Involvement in the Occult

Involvement in the occult can also be an open door for evil. This is why participation, or experimentation, in this area is so dangerous. Involvement in the occult could include divination, magic, spiritism, or combinations of these. Divination embraces such things as the Ouija board, tarot cards, astrology, fortune-telling, palm reading, rod and pendulum, water witching, psychometry, predicting dreams and visions, and crystal balls.

Occult magic is not the sleight of hand tricks or illusions which make bunny rabbits appear out of empty hats. Occult magic includes detectable phenomena produced by demonic forces such as the inflicting of pain, love and hate magic, curses, fertility charms, persecution and defense spells. Pharaoh's magicians utilized the power of demons for their anti-God purposes and so will the Antichrist. Divination concerns itself with the area of knowledge, while magic concerns itself with the area of power.

Spiritism involves the attempt to contact supernatural spirits or the spirits of dead people. Individuals often participate in spiritism to discover how their departed loved ones are doing in the other world. Others participate in order to attain some advantage or personal gain.

God strictly prohibits this type of activity in the Old Testament as seen in Leviticus 19:31 and Deuteronomy 18:10-12. King Saul died not only for the sin of rebellion, but also for the sin of consulting a medium as 1 Chronicles 10:13-14 indicates. God condemns this practice in other Old Testament passages as well: 2 Kin. 21:6; 23:24; 2 Chron. 33:6; Is. 8:19; 47:9-14.

Involvement in the occult, whether by habitual practice or through experimentation, opens a door for demonic involvement. Questioning counselees about occult involvement should be standard procedure in determining if one is demonically oppressed.

Ancestral Sin

Revealing their scientific worldview, many find it hard to believe that ancestral sin can also be an entry point for Satan's work. However, this reality is based both on theology and experience. If one's parents or ancestors were involved in the occult and experienced demonic activity, then the children and ancestors may also be affected by that experience.

Fred Dickason, in his book *Demon Possession and the Christian,* states that the majority of persons to whom he has ministered unto have had some measure of bondage due to ancestral sin.[5] At the time of publication, Dickason had seen over 400 persons with 95% of them experiencing demonization because of some ancestral involvement in occult activities. He believes this is a major cause of demonization.

In addition to experiences like Fred Dickason's, the consequences of ancestral sin is both possible and Scripturally defensible, i.e. Ex. 20:5-6; 34:7; Lev. 26:39-43; Jer. 32:18; Lam. 5:7.

Jeremiah 32:18 states that God shows lovingkindness to thousands, but repays the iniquity of fathers into the bosom of their children after them. This occurred with the descendants of Jeroboam. Because he did more evil than all who went before him, God promised to dispose of his male descendants in Israel (1 Kin.14:9-10). This came true in 1 Kings 15 as all the males of Jeroboam's household were killed by Baasha.

The same judgment came upon Baasha in 1 Kings 16:1-3. We see the principle played out in the corporate life of Israel as Jeremiah 16:10-13 declares that they were removed from the promised land because of their own sin and the sins of their forefathers. Nehemiah recognized this as he stated in Nehemiah 9:33-37:

> *In all that has happened to us, you have been just; you have acted faithfully, while we did wrong. Our kings, our leaders, our priests and our fathers did not follow your law; they did not pay attention to your commands or the warnings you gave them. Even while they were in their kingdom, enjoying your great goodness to them in the spacious and fertile land you gave them, they did not serve you or turn from their evil ways. But see, we are slaves today, slaves in the land you gave our forefathers so they could eat its fruit and the other good things it produces. Because of our sins, its abundant harvest goes to the kings you have placed over us. They rule over our bodies and our cattle as they please. We are in great distress.* (NIV)

Jesus himself seems to apply this principle in His caustic warnings to the Scribes and Pharisees in Matthew 23:32-36:

> *Fill up the measure of the guilt of your fathers. You serpents, you brood of vipers, how shall you escape the sentence of hell? Therefore, behold, I am sending you prophets and wise men and scribes; some of them you will kill and crucify, and some of them you will scourge in your synagogues, and persecute from city to city, that upon you may fall the guilt of all the righteous blood shed on earth, from the blood of righteous Abel to the blood of Zechariah, the son of Berechiah, who you murdered between the temple and the altar. Truly I say to you, all these things shall come upon this generation.*

Romans 1:21-32 describes the rebelliousness of humankind and its descent into idolatry. In judgment, God gave them over to further sin. The consequences of sin upon the third and fourth generations is a real possibility in light of these actions.

We have no problem accepting this principle in the physical

realm. Why is it so hard to accept in the spiritual realm? A child born to drug addicted parents may come into the world with a chemical dependency on those drugs for which he/she has absolutely no responsibility. The child is a victim of the parents' sin. It is readily accepted that children who are victims of emotional abuse have a greater tendency to become abusive parents themselves.

The same principle applies in the spiritual realm. Demons claim that if a parent gave them ground through unconfessed sin, they have a right to harass the offspring of that person. This does not make the child guilty of the parent's sin, for individuals are responsible for their own sins. However, it does mean that demonic strongholds through ancestral sin is a very real possibility both theologically and experientially.

Find The Point of Entry

The difficulty with ancestral sin is not the resolution of the issue, for that is quite simple. The difficulty arises from a lack of recognition by pastors, counselors, and concerned others. Either they are not aware that this possibility exists, or they do not believe it to be true.

If the open door through which demonic spirits have entered is not recognized as needing to be closed, shutting the door becomes more difficult. Once the entry point has been identified, resolution involves the following: 1) confessing sin; 2) renouncing Satan and any stronghold he claims through that sin; 3) claiming the truth about one's position, identity, power, and benefits in the Cross.

I remember teaching on spiritual warfare during a Wednesday evening Bible Study. People sneered, rolled their eyes, and looked upon me in disgust that I would teach such a thing. It had never happened to them, it did not fit well with their perception of reality, so they dismissed it as another pastoral blunder. They had no idea that during the previous Saturday I spent the better part of the day leading one of their fellow parishioners through steps to freedom from demonic bondage. One of those important steps involved renouncing her grandmother's past involvement in the occult.

Experiencing freedom from demonic control and harassment for the first time, this individual said to me, "I'm so glad I finally found someone who knows what to do." To dismiss this aspect of spiritual warfare is to miss golden opportunities for ministry.

The major causes of demonization are personal sin, both past and present, involvement in the occult either by participation or experimentation, and ancestral sin. There are other entry points for demonic strongholds such as the use of drugs, associations with false religions, satanic rock groups, etc. Discovering Satan's entry point allows us to uncover his deception.

The Flesh, the World, and Satan

Often, I encounter individuals claiming to be oppressed by Satan and demons when the real issue is a lack of disciplining the flesh. Believers struggle with battles apart from Satan and his demons; battles that result from the flesh and the world. The devil obviously uses the flesh and the world to his advantage, but they are not necessarily the direct result of demonic oppression.

A man in his twenties came to me for counseling because he was unable to control his thoughts and actions regarding lust. It soon became apparent that direct demonic oppression was not involved and the problem was elsewhere.

Digging deeper into the matter, it became evident that this individual was not allowing his new man to rule over his flesh. There were no demons that "made him do it." It was a matter of discipline and appropriating what had already been accomplished for him.

As I began to discuss the real issue behind the problem, he rolled his eyes in boredom, stared out the window, and felt the discussion was fruitless.

In short, he was desperately looking for a quick fix. Finding a demon behind his problem meant less work on his part. I was asking him to bring his desires and thoughts under the control of the Holy Spirit. It was easier for him to blame Satan than exercise the discipline of the Spirit. Not everything we face is a direct attack by demonic powers.

The Flesh

At the moment of conversion, our relationship with sin was severed as we no longer were slaves under the bondage of sin. But just because we are no longer under sin's bondage, does not mean that sin's existence is terminated. Sin is still alive, strong, and sometimes appealing, but its power and authority over us has been broken as stated in Romans 8:2, "For the law of the Spirit of life in Christ Jesus has set you free from the law of sin and of death."

Furthermore, it is true that our old sinful man has now been replaced with a new man who desires to follow after God. Despite this wonderful truth, it is still possible, as a matter of choice, to walk according to the flesh as Romans 8:12-13 indicates:

> *So then, brethren, we are under obligation, not to the flesh, to live according to the flesh, for if you are living according to the flesh, you must die; but if by the Spirit you are putting to death the deeds of the body, you will live.*

If our flesh is the problem, then blaming a direct assault by Satan and his demons is unnecessary. Although the old man has been crucified, it is the responsibility of individual believers to crucify the flesh and allow the new man to rule. Paul clearly informs us of this in Romans 6:12-14:

> *Therefore do not let sin reign in your mortal body that you should obey its lusts, and do not go on presenting the members of your body to sin as instruments of unrighteousness; but present yourselves to God as those alive from the dead, and your members as instruments of righteousness to God. For sin shall not be master over you, for you are not under law, but under grace.*

Presenting the members of our body to God as instruments of righteousness is our responsibility. Additionally, Romans 12:1-2 instructs us to renew our mind and present ourselves as living sacrifices as a form of worship to God:

I urge you therefore, brethren, by the mercies of God, to present your bodies a living and holy sacrifice, acceptable to God, which is your spiritual service of worship. And do not be conformed to this world, but be transformed by the renewing of your mind, that you may prove what the will of God is, that which is good and acceptable and perfect.

In Galatians 5, Paul details the difference between walking according to the Spirit and walking according to the flesh. Walking in the flesh is such a serious matter that he warns the Galatians in verse 21 that "those who practice such things shall not inherit the kingdom of God." While Satan can directly attack believers, succumbing to the flesh may be a simple matter of not yielding the members of our body to the control and influence of the Spirit.

Envisioning more than a physical body, the flesh (sarx) encompasses our mind, emotions, imagination, and will. All of this is housed in a physical body of flesh and blood which, for some, has been trained for years in unrighteousness. One day we will receive new bodies, perfect for enjoying the splendor of heaven. For now, we walk in the Spirit by yielding the members of our body (i.e. physical, emotional, intellectual, etc.) to God.

If the problem is our flesh, the solution is walking according to the Spirit. This involves renewing our mind, being filled with the Holy Spirit, and presenting the members of our body for the glory of God. It does not involve casting out demons.

Succumbing to the flesh is not necessarily a demonic attack, but *habitual indulgence* in the desires of the flesh can lead to demonic bondage. If one lives according to the flesh too long, the issues of sin may create a stronghold for Satan and his demons. If demonic bondage does occur, it is necessary for the individual to confess and forsake sin, renounce Satan, claim the victory of Christ, and reclaim lost ground.

Freedom from demonic bondage can come about instantly and immediately, but spiritual growth and maturity take time. Discipleship is a growth process. Freeing someone from Satan's stronghold provides opportunity to pursue a godly lifestyle without the hassle of Satanic oppression.

A Sinful World System

Our battle with the flesh is aggravated by the world system in which we live. Even though our citizenship is in heaven, we dwell on Earth as aliens and strangers (Eph. 2:19; Phil. 3:20; Heb. 11:13; 1 Pet. 2:11). 1 John 2:15 states, "Do not love the world, nor the things in the world. If anyone loves the world, the love of the Father is not in him."

Jesus reminded His disciples in John 15:19, "If you were of the world, the world would love its own; but because you are not of the world, but I chose you out of the world, therefore the world hates you." This world is not a friendly place for the followers of Christ.

The world which opposes the children of God is made up of people, attitudes, philosophies, governments, and the like which set themselves in direct opposition to God. Satan works to create a corrupt world which appeals to our flesh. It is designed to tempt us into sin and produce behavior which does not glorify God.

Furthermore, 1 John 2:16 states, "For all that is in the world, the lust of the flesh and the lust of the eyes and the boastful pride of life, is not from the Father, but is from the world." Since Satan is portrayed as the prince of this fallen environment (Jn. 12:31; 2 Cor. 4:4), it is easy to see his orchestration behind this evil environment.

Satan attempts to create a fertile atmosphere which elevates and promotes the sins of the flesh in order to lead us into bondage. He wants to surround us with what our flesh desires. This is why yielding our flesh to the control of the Holy Spirit is so essential.

We face this type of temptation every day of the week. The world lures us after its glittering, sparkling gifts. When the package is unwrapped, however, the glitter and dazzle fades into sin and the consequential price tag is extremely high.

The world can be overcome through our faith according to 1 John 5:4-5:

> *For whatever is born of God overcomes the world; and this is the victory that has overcome the world, our faith. And who is the one who overcomes the world, but he who believes that Jesus is the Son of God?*

Faith simply means "belief" and is used as both a noun and a verb. As a noun, it refers to the whole body of revealed truth which has come to us by the revelation of God. We overcome the world when we assimilate this truth into our life through reading, memorizing, and understanding the Word of God. The more we familiarize ourselves with Scripture, the easier it is to correctly assess and overcome the world's deceptive offers.

As a verb, faith refers to our personal application and appropriation of the victory through our Lord Jesus Christ. It is not only a body of knowledge that we agree is true, its truth is also actively applied to our lives. We not only believe it, we live it.

Jesus states, in John 16:33, that He has overcome the world, "In the world you have tribulation, but take courage; I have overcome the world." We experience victory because Christ is victorious over the world. Personal victory includes not only an understanding of God's revealed truth known as Scripture, but also the personal appropriation of Christ's victory to our lives.

Although Satan is ultimately behind all evil, not every problem we encounter is a direct assault by the rebel prince. There are other areas we should examine such as our flesh and the sinful environment in which we live. While a distinction between the flesh, the world, and the devil proves helpful, a note of caution is needed. Our scientific worldview likes to categorize, analyze, and place everything in neat little compartments. In reality, the lines of distinction are often blurred. The flesh, the world, and the devil, are often mingled together in such a way that makes separation difficult.

F O U R

STRATEGIC BATTLEFIELDS

Christians can be subtly deceived in the inner chambers of their mind. Since it is not an obvious evil, they do not recognize how even the smallest deception influences their behavior in an ungodly direction.

The art of deception begins in the mind. Satan, who is a chronic liar, is determined to trick us into believing his deceptive lies so we will behave in a manner which detracts from the glory of God.

The Bible vehemently depicts Satan as a liar, and Jesus even speaks of this in John 8:44 saying:

> *You are of your father the devil, and you want to do the desires of your father. He was a murderer from the beginning, and does not stand in the truth, because there is no truth in him. Whenever he speaks a lie, he speaks from his own nature; for he is a liar, and the father of lies.*

It is interesting to note that Jesus spoke these words to deceived Jews who believed that because Abraham was their father, their relationship with God was secure.

The dishonest nature of Satan is further seen in Revelation 12:9:

> *And the great dragon was thrown down, the serpent of old who is called the devil and Satan, who deceives the whole world; he was thrown down to the earth, and his angels were thrown down with him.*

Satan is an absolute liar. There is no truth in him. He lies in order to deceive. If Satan can deceive our mind, that is, what we think and believe is true, then he can control our actions, because our mind directs our behavior.

His strategy and pattern of lying has been around a very long time. He sprang his artful lie upon Eve in the Garden of Eden. He suggested that God was withholding something good from her. After all, he implied, why would God withhold the pleasure of delicious fruit? Could it be that God wanted to keep her from experiencing the valuable benefits and pleasures associated with eating from the forbidden tree? Satan implied that God's motives were impure and that He did not have her best interest at heart.

Eve wrestled with these deceptive thoughts Satan brought to her mind, when in reality, the opposite of what he suggested was true. God did have her best interest at heart. He was not at all attempting to withhold something valuable, pleasurable, and good from her. Eve's mind became the battlefield where Satan launched his attack. Once she swallowed the bait, he won the battle and influenced her behavior in an ungodly direction.

Recognizing the deceptive handiwork of Satan in the minds of unprepared believers, Paul wrote to the church in Corinth (2 Cor. 11:3), "But I am afraid, lest as the serpent deceived Eve by his craftiness, your minds should be led astray from the simplicity and purity of devotion to Christ."

In Romans 1:25, Paul describes those apart from Christ as people who "exchanged the truth of God for a lie, and worshiped and served the creature rather than the Creator..."

Before we came to Christ, we were also deceived by blinding lies as Ephesians 2:3 notes, "Among them we too all formerly lived in the lusts of our flesh, indulging the desires of the flesh and of the mind, and we were by nature children of wrath, even as the rest." Colossians 1:21 further states that we were at one time alienated and hostile "in mind" against God.

Most everything we do begins as a thought in our mind. This is why Paul says, in Romans 8:6-7:

> *For the mind set on the flesh is death, but the mind set on the Spirit is life and peace, because the mind set on the flesh is hostile toward God, for it does not subject itself to the law of God, for it is not even able to do so.*

Since the mind is the control room which triggers our behavior, victorious Christian living and successful spiritual warfare compels us to set our mind on the things of God and guard it with great vigilance. One of Satan's most effective methods of controlling our behavior is deceiving our mind. He does this through the web of lies he continually spins. He knows that if we will believe them, he can successfully entice us to sin in the same manner as his success with Eve in the Garden of Eden.

The smug attitude often displayed by many Christians is, "I have been a Christian for years and there is no way I could be deceived like Eve." This kind of statement indicates that one is already deceived in their understanding of Satan's shrewd ability.

Additionally, many Christians submit to the fallacy that spiritual warfare only involves weird things, the far out extremes of the occult, and the obvious evil, when in reality spiritual warfare happens all around us in subtle and unexpected ways.

Christians can be subtly deceived in the inner chambers of their mind. Since it is not an obvious evil, they do not recognize how even the smallest deception influences their behavior in an ungodly direction.

One does not have to belong to the occult to be under demonic control. The stark reality of the situation suggests that the extent a person is controlled and influenced by Satan is proportionate to the extent they knowingly or unknowingly believe his deceptive lies.

It is entirely possible for a believer to attend church every time the doors are open, be a faithful contributor, and even maintain a position of leadership and still be unwittingly under the influence of Satan and hindering a local church from glorifying God to its fullest potential. Someone who does not believe they can be deceived, actually is deceived. Satan is certainly a tricky devil!

The unbeliever, who is already in Satan's kingdom, has only one lie to believe, that Jesus' death and resurrection is insignificant and irrelevant. Since Satan already has unbelievers in his camp, his primary targets are believers who desire to live for the Lord.

In an all out attempt to keep us in a state of spiritual ineffectiveness, he tries to deceive our mind in subtle and unnoticeable ways so he can control our behavior without us ever suspecting his involvement. This is the old "angel of light" trick as noted in 2 Corinthians 11:14, "Satan disguises himself as an angel of light."

Environmental Stimuli

Even though we are children of God with the promised hope of heaven, we still must live on Earth until that promise is fulfilled. We are strangers and aliens in this world because our true citizenship is in heaven (Phil. 3:20; 1 Pet. 2:11). Until we get to heaven, the environment we live in provides Satan with a great arsenal of evil stimulation to bring before our eyes and ears.

Having observed us throughout the years, he is keenly aware of our weak areas of vulnerability. He uses this fallen environment to negatively stimulate our thoughts and tempt us into ungodly behavior which does not bring glory to our Heavenly Father.

The books we read, the music we listen to, the television shows we watch, and the events we participate in, can have a positive or negative influence upon our spiritual walk. What we do, and where we spend our time, whether it is only for a brief moment or for an extended period, can have a huge impact upon our thoughts. When our mind is stimulated to concentrate on the good things (Phil. 4:8), we honor God and are less likely to succumb to temptation.

Actions Begin as Thoughts

Just how important the mind is during temptation is illustrated in a "Cathy" cartoon strip. Without exercising control over our thoughts, deception is free to accomplish its dirty work. While struggling with her diet, Cathy succumbs to the temptation by allowing her thoughts to go unchecked and unchallenged.

Frame 1: I will take a drive, but won't go near the grocery store.
Frame 2: I will drive by the grocery store, but will not go in it.
Frame 3: I will go in the grocery store, but will not walk down the aisle where the Halloween candy is on sale.

Frame 4: I will look at the candy, but not pick it up.
Frame 5: I will pick it up, but not buy it.
Frame 6: I will buy it, but not open it.
Frame 7: Open it, but not smell it.
Frame 8: Smell it, but not taste it.
Frame 9: Taste it, but not eat it.
Frame 10: *Eat, eat, eat, eat, eat!*

When David observed Bathsheba bathing (2 Sam. 11), he had the opportunity to turn and make a deliberate choice not to look. Instead, he lingered, and rather than turning away in frame one, frame ten ended with adultery and murder. To hesitate in frame one increases the odds that we will wind up in frame ten.

Realizing that the mind is fertile soil for spiritual warfare, the Bible cautions us over and over to guard it and keep our thoughts focused on the things of God. It does not take long for a behavior to become a habit. Repeating an action for six weeks will enforce its habitual nature upon us. Once it becomes a habit, it can easily develop into a stronghold for Satan.

To say that I was stunned when I first discovered that Satan could actually put thoughts in my mind is an enormous understatement. Issues of spiritual warfare finally began to make more sense to me. With the typical response of those who have just realized they were deceived, I exclaimed, "Why did I not see this before?" I was easy prey. By definition of the term, deception would not be deception if the person realized it.

The following verses reveal that Satan can put deceptive thoughts in our mind:

1 Chronicles 21:1

Then Satan stood up against Israel and moved David to number Israel.

John 13:2

And during supper, the devil having already put into the heart of Judas Iscariot, the son of Simon, to betray Him.

Acts 5:3

> *But Peter said, Ananias, why has Satan filled your heart to lie to the Holy Spirit, and to keep back some of the price of the land?*

Just how does this deception of the mind take place? Does Satan sit down in a face-to-face talk and say, "Oh, by the way David, I want you to number Israel," or "Hey Judas, I think it would be a good idea if you betrayed Jesus. He wouldn't like it very much and it will ultimately lead to His death, but you would make a little spending money."

The way Satan tricked them is the same way he tricks us. Our temptations do not come through a face-to-face dinner table discussion with Satan. Our temptations arise from thoughts in our mind and Satan has the ability to put them there!

The idea of numbering Israel was an evil thought placed in the mind of David. Thoughts of Judas betraying Jesus, and Ananias lying about the price of land, originated with Satan. He put those thoughts in their minds. During the wilderness temptation, Satan filled Jesus' mind with many tempting thoughts. However, we find Jesus combatting these thoughts with Scripture and resisting any thought of acting upon the temptation.

While completing my doctoral degree, I enrolled in a spiritual warfare course. In the dorm room, sleep evaded me because of reoccurring wicked and vile thoughts. Prior to the course, I would have mentally beat myself up saying, "Wow, how can I, as a minister of God, think these sort of things? I am not a very good Christian." The course, however, taught me that not all my thoughts were my own, since Satan has the ability to place them into my mind. Recognizing that the enemy was attempting to deceive me into sinful behavior, I took swift action against the evil thoughts and was no longer bothered.

This simple concept has had an emancipating affect upon many whom I have counseled. Before realizing this truth, they would take a spiritual baseball bat and club themselves over the head countless times for even thinking a bad thought. But as we have noted, there is no sin in the initial thought. If there was, Jesus would have been a sinner for even thinking about Satan's temptations during the wilderness experience. Jesus must have processed the temptation through His mind, otherwise He would not have been able to comprehend and respond to it.

Those initial thoughts become sin when we dwell on them and turn them into ungodly behavior. When a tempting thought entered Jesus' mind such as worshipping Satan, He quickly responded with Scripture, turned away, and refused to have anything to do with ungodly behavior. Lingering upon an evil thought ends in trouble.

Satan is the biggest con man around and he wants us to believe that every thought we think is ours, not his. He attempts to control us with his deceptive lies and make us feel horrible for even having such a thought. Without deception, Satan is powerless. In other words, Satan's only hold over us is in an area where he has successfully deceived us. When we expose his deceptive lies to the truth of God's Word, his power is broken.

Satan's predicament reminds me of a person with dentures eating steak. Take out the dentures and they have no ability to bite. In a similar vein, Satan's bite is without much strength when his deceptive lies are exposed.

Countering Lies With Truth

Since Satan's main strategy is deceiving Christians into believing his lies, our main strategy directly counters this tactic. We utilize the truth of God's Word as our weapon. Jesus said, in John 8:32, "and you shall know the truth, and the truth shall make you free." As a powerful searchlight, truth exposes dark deception.

Jesus utilized the powerful Word of God during His temptations in the wilderness. When Satan tempted Him with an evil thought, Jesus brought the light of Scripture into the picture and Satan could progress no further. He was forced to abandon the lie and try an alternate route.

In light of Hebrews 4:12, we should never underestimate the power of Scripture:

For the word of God is living and active and sharper than any two-edged sword, and piercing as far as the division of soul and spirit, of both joints and marrow, and able to judge the thoughts and intentions of the heart.

Distorting Truth

Satan's jealous nature propels him toward distorting the truth about God in any possible way. While tempting Eve in the Garden of Eden, he maligned the character of God by insinuating that He was withholding good from her.

In a similar approach, the devil distorts the truth about God by pawning off inaccurate caricatures of Him. Satan makes God out to be a vindictive judge who revels in our mistakes, just waiting for us to do something wrong in order to make us suffer.

He also portrays God as a demanding parent who is difficult to please. We had better receive A's on our spiritual report card and prove our worth to Him or we are in big trouble. God is also characterized as the universal policeman out to spoil our fun just so He can write us a ticket. In an age of divorce and abuse, the devil also enjoys equating our Heavenly Father with corrupt earthly fathers.

By attacking the foundational truth of God, he influences everything else affected by that view, which is virtually everything. The degree to which we believe or act upon Satan's lies, is the degree to which he has control over us.

Satan also loves to distort what is good by extending it beyond appropriate boundaries, until it becomes sin. For example, self-respect is good, but taken too far becomes conceit. Generosity is good, but taken too far becomes wastefulness. Physical rest is good, but taken too far becomes laziness. Communication is good, but taken too far becomes gossip.

Steps For Winning the Battle

How do we go about destroying these strongholds and defeating Satan on the battlefield of the mind?

First, being transformed by the renewing of our minds is absolutely essential according to Romans 12:2:

> *And do not be conformed to this world, but be transformed by the renewing of your mind, that you may prove what the will of God is, that which is good and acceptable and perfect.*

We renew our mind by filling it with God's Word. Colossians 3:16 exhorts us to, "let the word of Christ richly dwell within you..." The Psalmist boldly declares in 119:11, "Thy word I have treasured in my heart, that I may not sin against Thee."

Familiarization with Scripture produces an arsenal of truth weapons to utilize against the enemy. A consistent study of the Bible is essential for victory on the battlefield of the mind, for if we are unfamiliar with the truth of God's Word, it becomes difficult to recognize a deceptive lie.

I remember hearing a story about Billy Graham's wife, Ruth, as she was visiting Scotland Yard's counterfeit money division. Mrs. Graham mentioned that it must take a great deal of time and effort to familiarize oneself with the forgeries in order to distinguish it from the real money.

To her astonishment, Scotland Yard professionals informed her that the very opposite was true. In order to recognize the counterfeit money, they spend their time familiarizing themselves with the real money. The same principle applies in the spiritual realm. Familiarization with the truth of God's Word helps us recognize Satan's counterfeit diversions.

Preparing our minds for action is a necessary second step as noted in 1 Peter 1:13, "Therefore, gird your minds for action." Becoming a Christian does not automatically place our brain in neutral. Instead of allowing critical thinking to fall by the wayside, Christians are actually told to engage their minds. Immediately after admonishing us to prepare our minds, Peter warns us in the following verse not to be conformed to our former lusts. In other words, a prepared mind restrains sinful behavior.

One of the churches I pastored contained a large gymnasium of which the church basketball team made regular use. On countless occasions, either I or someone else, forfeited an easy bucket because of a mental lapse in readiness. A man drives the lane and two opponents quickly cut him off leaving me open under the basket. My teammate dishes me the ball for an easy score but it slips out of my hands and out of bounds. I became lazy in my mind, not anticipating what was to come. My dulled mental alertness became an advantage for the other team.

In a similar manner, Satan takes advantage of our mental lapses of readiness, just waiting for us to drop the ball. Is our mind sharp to the things of God? Are we mentally ready and prepared for both the moving of God and the schemes of the enemy?

Taking every thought captive to the obedience of Christ is the third battlefield tactic. This is exactly the technique I employed during my doctoral class on spiritual warfare when I was mentally bombarded with evil thoughts. It follows the advice of 2 Corinthians 10:3-5:

> *For though we walk in the flesh, we do not war according to the flesh, for the weapons of our warfare are not of the flesh, but divinely powerful for the destruction of fortresses. We are destroying speculations and every lofty thing raised up against the knowledge of God, and we are taking every thought captive to the obedience of Christ.*

When thoughts enter our mind, an evaluation process ensues. If the thought aligns with what is right and pure in the eyes of God, then we should accept it. If the thought is impure, then we should reject it by taking it captive to the obedience of Christ. Cathy, the cartoon strip character, would have won her battle over eating candy had she taken the thought captive in the first frame.

Thoughts taken captive to the obedience of Christ are harnessed under the searchlight of the Holy Spirit. Realizing that every thought we think does not necessarily originate with ourselves, we do not want uncontrolled or loose thoughts running around in our mind. Either verbally or mentally say, "This thought is not of God, therefore I take it captive to the obedience of Christ."

Satan has a difficult time gaining strongholds in our thought life when an alert mind quickly exposes his lies and deception. Our mind is not the property of Satan and we have the right to restrain those evil thoughts, take them captive, and experience victory in the secret chambers of our mind.

The fourth strategic battlefield tactic is thinking on those things which are true, honorable, right, pure, of good repute, and anything excellent and worthy of praise of which Philippians 4:8-9 instructs:

> *Finally, brethren, whatever is true, whatever is honorable, whatever is right, whatever is pure, whatever is lovely, whatever is of good repute, if there is excellence and if anything worthy of praise, let your mind dwell on these things. The things you have learned and received and heard and seen in me, practice these things; and the God of peace shall be with you.*

If we do this, verse nine assures us that the peace of God will be with us. The more our minds dwell on good things, those things which are spiritually healthy for us, the less likely we are to think evil thoughts, and act upon them.

By adhering to these four strategic battlefield tactics for the mind, victory is experienced to a greater degree:

1. Renew our minds by the transformation of Christ. (Rom. 12:2)

2. Keep our mind spiritually alert and prepared for the moving of God and the deceptive schemes of the enemy. (1 Pet. 1:13)

3. Take all thoughts captive to the obedience of Christ. (2 Cor. 10:3-5)

4. Keep our mind actively thinking on the things of God. (Phil. 4:8-9)

The Battle Over Identity

The issue of our identity in Christ is another major battleground in which Satan rings believers like a wet rag. Sadly enough, the devil scores needless victories in this area when a correct and biblical view of identity could knock him to the canvas quickly and easily.

After numerous years in pastoral ministry, it has been my experience that many believers struggle with their Christian identity. Yet, if they can nail this issue down with clarity and confidence, they will find a stable platform for fighting the battle.

Pondering the staggering implications of our relationship with Jesus is a worthwhile activity. When was the last time you sat down and really thought about who you are?

Far too often, believers go through life bound to an old way of thinking about themselves. They live in the past of what they once were, instead of what they are now as redeemed children of God. Satan knows that if we realize the richness of our position in Christ, we become a powerful foe and a major threat to his evil operations.

Who Are You?

People tend to identify themselves by the following methods:

Name
Address
Profession
Nationality
Denomination
Physical Characteristics

But do these characteristics really represent who we are? Our name only reveals what others call us. Our profession only informs others what we do for a living. Our nationality only reveals that we belong to a certain nation. Our address merely reveals where we live. Our denomination only communicates our particular religious affiliation. Our physical characteristics only make known our height, weight, and external features.

Yet, most Americans identify themselves by name and occupation. Most Christians identify themselves by their denominational preference and their doctrinal viewpoint (charismatic, pentecostal, evangelical, mainline, reformed, dispensational, etc.).

All of these identifying factors fall short of expressing who we really are in Christ, because our true identity is not grounded upon what we do, where we live, what we look like, or what denomination we prefer. Incorrect thinking believes that our identity is based on what we do. In other words, what I do determines who I am. But this is backwards. As you will soon see, quite the opposite is true. In reality, what we do is determined by who we are. Satan gains a strategic advantage when believers misconstrue the power of their identity in Christ.

The Identity Equation

Our society associates happiness, wholeness, and self-esteem with good looks, the right relationships, and a large stock portfolio. Without these items, they say happiness is a fleeting dream and life becomes hopeless and meaningless.

While I certainly do not consider myself homely (although some may disagree!), I will never be asked to model the best selling magazine for men's attire. The admirable square jaw needed for success eludes me. I might have a chance if the round chipmunk face were in vogue. Yet, despite my lack of a model physique, I am amazingly happy.

I have no large stock portfolio and I do not manipulate relationships for the sake of climbing to the top, yet I am remarkably happy. The world is quite surprised at this. Since I do not possess what they value, how can there be happiness in my life? They fail to realize that happiness is not the sum of things, money, and manipulation. When the wrong equation for happiness is employed, the wrong conclusion will be reached.

Of all people, Christians have a solid reason for rejoicing. In God's kingdom the equation for happiness looks like this:

ME + CHRIST = COMPLETENESS

Wholeness, happiness, and meaning to life is derived from a personal relationship with Jesus Christ, not by the number of rooms in our house. Identity relates to spiritual warfare because Satan, in an effort to restrain our ability to glorify God, distorts our perception of who we are in Christ so he can influence our behavior.

Inverted Thinking

Inverted thinking is when we have things backwards or upside down. It is believing that we are nothing, when God says we are something. It is believing the devil's lies about ourselves, instead of believing the truth of God's Word. Greater happiness, greater impact, and greater victory is experienced when inverted thinking is corrected and one's identity is allowed to influence behavior.

Please do not underestimate the significance of this issue! Our perception of who we are influences how we act and react. For example, if we perceive that we are insignificant and unable to do much for God, then we will live a powerless Christian life. If we merely think of ourselves as dirty no good sinners, then we will likely behave that way.

The point is this, people do not behave in a manner that is inconsistent with the way they perceive themselves. While they may be able to fool others for awhile, their self-perceptions are revealed by how they act over time. Who we are is not determined by what we do, rather, what we do is determined by who we are. The difference this truth can make in our spiritual walk is priceless.

The entire book of Ephesians emphasizes this very point. The first half of the Epistle discusses the theological truth about a believer's position in Christ, while the second half of the Epistle admonishes us to live out our new redeemed identity. In light of the fact that we are saved totally by the grace of God, apart from any meritorious work on our part (Eph. 2:8-9; Titus 3:5-7), we engage in spiritual work not to *become* children of God, but because we *already are* children of God.

Rather than being underdogs in an uphill race struggling to gain a position against the enemy, the book of Ephesians portrays us as God's elect, engaging the enemy from an advantageous position of strength and victory. For too long we have been riding the train that downs us, belittles us, and causes us to question our worth, value, and impact in God's kingdom. It is time to realize our powerful new redeemed identity, switch tracks, and engage the enemy from a strong position of confidence. A firm grasp of who we are in Christ can readily derail Satan's train of deception.

We Are Holy Saints

Throughout the book of Ephesians, there are over 40 references to being in Christ and having Christ in us. Being a follower of Jesus Christ is not just a matter of *getting* something; it is a matter of *being* someone.

A long-time friend called me late one night and introduced himself as saint Greg. It was not said in jest or with an arrogant attitude. It was a firm affirmation of his new redeemed status. The core of our identity is not our occupation, our nationality, our denominational affiliation, or our physical appearance. The core of our identity is that we are saints, redeemed children of the holy, powerful, and living God.

The Bible does not refer to Christians as "sinners." According to Ephesians 2, Paul makes the point that although this is what we once were (past tense), that is not what we are now (present tense). Read the chapter! A sinner is what we were apart from Christ, but now we are a saint because of our relationship with the Savior.

Paul did not write his Ephesian letter to a group of sinners gathered in Ephesus, he wrote it "to the saints who are at Ephesus, and who are faithful in Christ Jesus." (Eph. 1:1). He uses this term frequently to describe the recipients of his letters who were faithful in Christ: 1 Corinthians, 2 Corinthians, Philippians, and Colossians.

Sometimes we wallow in a "poor little me" theology which reaffirms our lack of worth and utter sinfulness. Somehow we may think it is spiritual to pray to God constantly mentioning that we are merely sinners saved by grace.

As I have listened to this cliché being prayed by leaders in the church, I know they are simply attempting to give God glory for saving them, since they could not save themselves. However, I wonder how many of them live in the past instead of the present? It has been a very long time since I heard someone glorify God for turning them into a saint! Could it be possible that while acknowledging the truth of the past, Satan has deceived us about the power of the present?

Just because the Bible portrays believers as holy saints does not mean they can never sin. A quick examination of our lives reveals otherwise. Scripture even informs us that we will at times sin (1 Jn. 1:8,10). In such cases we are to quickly confess that sin unto the Lord (1 Jn. 1:9).

We are not referring to perfection but to our true perception of our identity. There is a difference in perception between the person who sees himself as a poor old dirty sinner barely saved by grace and the person who perceives himself as a saint who occasionally sins. Do you see how this perception could affect one's spiritual life? This is important because people act according to how they truly perceive themselves.

Satan wants us to believe that we are sinners because we sometimes sin. God wants us to believe that we are saints who sometimes sin. Satan wants us to receive our identity from what *we do,* but God wants us to receive our identity from what He *has done for us*. Satan wants us to base our identity on what *other people* say about us, but God wants us to receive our identity from what *He says about us*. Satan wants our behavior to determine our identity, but God wants our true identity in Him to determine our behavior.

In reference to our rich identity in Christ, the Bible has the following to say:

YOU ARE

A SAINT Eph. 1:1; 1 Cor. 1:2 ; Phil. 1:1; Col. 1:2

A NEW CREATION IN CHRIST 2 Cor. 5:17

A MEMBER OF THE PEOPLE OF GOD, A CHOSEN RACE, ROYAL PRIESTHOOD, HOLY NATION 1 Pet. 2:9-10

A CHILD OF GOD 1 Jn. 3:1-2

A FRIEND OF CHRIST Jn. 15:15

CHOSEN OF CHRIST TO BEAR HIS FRUIT Jn. 15:16

BLESSED WITH EVERY SPIRITUAL BLESSING Eph. 1:3

A JOINT-HEIR WITH CHRIST SHARING IN HIS INHERITANCE Rom. 8:17

A TEMPLE OF GOD WHERE THE HOLY SPIRIT DWELLS 1 Cor. 3:16; 6:19

THE WORKMANSHIP OF GOD Eph. 2:10

RIGHTEOUS AND HOLY Eph. 4:24

JUSTIFIED Rom. 5:1

FREE FROM CONDEMNATION Rom. 8:1

A CITIZEN OF HEAVEN Phil. 3:20

SEATED IN THE HEAVENLIES WITH CHRIST Eph. 2:6

DELIVERED FROM SATAN'S KINGDOM TO GOD'S KINGDOM Col. 1:13

A CHILD OF LIGHT, NOT OF DARKNESS 1 Thess. 5:5

AN ALIEN AND STRANGER IN THIS WORLD SINCE YOU BELONG TO GOD 1 Pet. 2:11

THE ENEMY OF SATAN 1 Pet. 5:8

The following "Results List" further delineates the outcome of our new identity in Christ:

RESULTS LIST

Rom. 5:1	YOU HAVE BEEN JUSTIFIED AND HAVE PEACE WITH GOD.
Rom. 5:5	THE LOVE OF GOD HAS BEEN POURED OUT WITHIN YOUR HEART.
Rom. 6:1-6	YOU ARE FREE FROM THE BONDAGE OF SIN.
Rom. 8:1	SINCE YOU ARE FREE FROM THE BONDAGE OF SIN, YOU WILL NOT EXPERIENCE THE CONDEMNATION OF GOD.
Rom. 8:28	ALL THINGS WORK FOR YOUR GOOD.
Rom. 8:29-30	YOU WILL ONE DAY BE GLORIFIED.
1 Cor. 2:12	YOU HAVE BEEN GIVEN THE HOLY SPIRIT SO YOU MIGHT FREELY KNOW THE THINGS OF GOD.
1 Cor. 2:16	YOU HAVE THE MIND OF CHRIST.
1 Cor. 3:9	YOU ARE GOD'S FELLOW WORKER.
1 Cor. 3:23	YOU BELONG TO CHRIST.
1 Cor. 6:20	YOU WERE BOUGHT WITH A PRICE.

1 Cor. 12:7 YOU WERE GIVEN AT LEAST ONE SPIRITUAL GIFT, POSSIBLY MORE.

2 Cor. 1:21-22; 5:5; Eph. 1:13-14 THE HOLY SPIRIT INDWELLS YOU AND HAS BEEN GIVEN TO YOU AS A PLEDGE OF WHAT IS TO COME.

2 Cor. 5:18-20 AS GOD'S AMBASSADOR, YOU HAVE BEEN GIVEN THE MINISTRY OF RECONCILIATION.

2 Cor. 5:21 YOU ARE THE RIGHTEOUSNESS OF GOD.

Gal. 2:20 YOU HAVE BEEN CRUCIFIED WITH CHRIST AND THE LIFE YOU NOW LIVE IS CHRIST LIVING IN YOU.

Gal. 4:1-7 GOD ADOPTED YOU AS HIS CHILD AND YOU ARE AN HEIR OF GOD.

Eph. 1:3 GOD HAS BLESSED YOU WITH EVERY SPIRITUAL BLESSING.

Eph. 1:4-8 GOD CHOSE YOU BEFORE THE FOUNDATION OF THE WORLD TO BE ADOPTED AS HIS CHILD. AS SUCH, HE HAS LAVISHED UPON YOU HIS TREMENDOUS GRACE.

Eph. 2:5 YOU WERE MADE ALIVE TOGETHER WITH CHRIST.

Eph. 2:6 YOU HAVE BEEN RAISED UP WITH CHRIST AND SEATED WITH HIM IN THE HEAVENLIES.

Eph. 2:18; 3:12; Heb. 4:16 YOU CAN APPROACH GOD WITH CONFIDENCE AND BOLDNESS.

Eph. 6:10-18	YOU HAVE BEEN GIVEN THE ARMOR OF GOD.
Col. 1:14	YOU HAVE REDEMPTION AND THE FORGIVENESS OF YOUR SINS.
Col. 2:7	YOU ARE FIRMLY ROOTED IN CHRIST AND ARE BEING BUILT UP IN HIM.
2 Tim. 1:7	YOU WERE GIVEN A SPIRIT OF POWER, LOVE, AND DISCIPLINE.
Heb. 2:11	CHRIST IS NOT ASHAMED TO CALL YOU BRETHREN.
1 Pet. 1:3-5	YOU HAVE A LIVING HOPE OF OBTAINING YOUR INHERITANCE WHICH GOD IS PROTECTING FOR YOU.
2 Pet. 1:3-4	GOD HAS GRANTED YOU EVERYTHING NEEDED TO LIVE A LIFE OF GODLINESS.

These lists could go on and on and you may have additional Scriptural passages to add. We are rich in Christ and if Satan can deceive our self-perception, then he can control and influence our behavior. Paul, in his Ephesian letter, almost begs believers to begin living out who they actually are in Christ.

Christ's Identity Is Questioned

The devil tried this very tactic upon Jesus during the wilderness temptation. In the first temptation recorded in Matthew 4:3, Satan said, "*if* you are the Son of God, command that these stones become bread." Now there is nothing wrong with turning stones into bread, after all, Jesus did far greater miracles than this during His earthly ministry such as raising people from the dead, turning water into wine, and feeding thousands of people with only a meager amount of bread.

The temptation is really an identity test, not an issue of stones and bread. Satan wanted Jesus to turn the stones into bread to *prove* that He really was the Messiah. After all, He was just beginning His public ministry and it would be disastrous to start out if the claim was really not true.

If Jesus was unsure about His identity as the Son of God, He might have turned the stones into bread to prove His messiahship. Satan does not want us to live out our identity; to be secure in who we are; to really behave in a manner consistent with the riches and power granted to us by virtue of our relationship with Christ.

To begin living according to our new identity as redeemed children of God would bring an immense amount of honor and glory to our Heavenly Father. By confusing, attacking, and creating misunderstanding about our spiritual self-perception, Satan circumvents the glory process. When he is successful and effective, we become unsuccessful and ineffective.

The Old and the New

Before we began to follow Christ, we were sinful, serving Satan, separated from God, and deserving of death. Our nature *before* we came to Christ is described in Ephesians 2:1-3 :

> *And you were dead in your trespasses and sins, in which you formerly walked according to the course of this world, according to the prince of the power of the air, of the spirit that is now working in the sons of disobedience. Among them we too all formerly lived in the lusts of our flesh, indulging the desires of the flesh and of the mind, and we were by nature children of wrath, even as the rest.*

Conversion, however, changed the very essence of our nature. According to 2 Peter 1:4 we have become "partakers of the divine nature." We are not the Divine Essence, but we partake of it by virtue of the Holy Spirit dwelling within us.

Ephesians 5:8 says, "You were formerly darkness, but now you are light in the Lord, walk as children of the light." Paul does not say we resembled darkness or we resembled light, Paul actually states that *we were* darkness and now *we are* light. 2 Corinthians 5:17 affirms this new status by stating that, "if any man is in Christ, he is a new creature; the old things passed away; behold new things have come."

The Bible refers to the person we were before, as the old self or old man. At the moment of conversion, our old self or old man which was characterized by sin, died according to Romans 6:6, "your old self was crucified with Him, that our body of sin might be done away with, that we should no longer be slaves to sin."

When our old self died, our new self came to life and is characterized by faith and dependence upon God. Galatians 2:20 proclaims this very truth:

> *I have been crucified with Christ; and it is no longer I who live, but Christ lives in me; and the life which I now live in the flesh I live by faith in the Son of God, who loved me, and delivered Himself up for me.*

Our old self had to die in order to sever our relationship and bondage to sin. Being a new creature in Christ does not mean that we are sinless, for 1 John 1:8 clearly states, "If we say we have no sin, we are deceiving ourselves, and the truth is not in us." But since our old self has been crucified and buried with Christ, we are no longer *bound* to sin as 1 John 2:1 declares, "My little children, I am writing these things to you that you may not sin."

The death of our old self officially ended our relationship with sin, but it did not end the existence of sin. Although Satan and sin are still around, the crucifixion of the old self means that the power of sin over us is broken and we are no longer under any obligation to serve sin, obey sin, or respond to it. The following verses support this wonderful truth:

Romans 6:7
For he who has died is freed from sin.

Romans 6:12
Therefore do not let sin reign in your mortal body that you should obey its lust.

Romans 6:14
For sin shall not be master over you, for you are not under law, but under grace.

I can attest from many years of counseling in pastoral ministry that Satan will endlessly attack one's new redeemed identity in Christ. He will do all he can to bring confusion, misunderstanding, misinformation, and an "Oh, you're not good enough," mentality to undermine our ministry effectiveness. To misunderstand one's position in Christ is to give the enemy an edge, whereas a true appraisal of our new redeemed status prevents deception in this crucial area.

F I V E

THE ARMOR OF GOD

A warrior without armor is like a field mouse without cover. The hawk easily sweeps down and carries it away. A proper understanding and utilization of our protective armor makes for mighty warriors.

The armor which God graciously provides to believers in their battle with Satan is often misunderstood and almost always under-utilized. Failure to properly appropriate God's protective battle gear keeps us vulnerable and weakens our chance of successfully overcoming the enemy.

Before graduating from college, I attended a technical school to learn the welding trade. Leather welding capes protected the body from flying sparks and molten metal. Overhead welding is a tricky skill to master. Because gravity pulls the molten metal downward toward the body, this is definitely the time when a protective leather cape should be used. Since they were a bit pricey, I tried to get by with wearing three layers of clothing. It did not take me long to learn my lesson.

One day a red hot bead of metal dropped onto my sweatshirt, burned through three layers of clothing, wiggled down my pants and set my underwear on fire before coming to rest in my shoe. Believe me, there is not an NFL running back alive who could have kept pace with my speedy movements that day. A flaming body tends to motivate one toward quickness. Needless to say, the next day I purchased a protective leather welding cape.

The armor of God is similar to the cape's protective nature. Without it, we not only expose ourselves to needless danger, but fighting fires diverts our energies from more significant activities.

This armor is described in Ephesians 6:10-17:

Finally, be strong in the Lord, and in the strength of His might. Put on the full armor of God, that you may be able to stand firm against the schemes of the devil. For out struggle is not against flesh and blood, but against the rulers, against the powers, against the world forces of this darkness, against the spiritual forces of wickedness in the heavenly places. Therefore, take up the full armor of God, that you may be able to resist in the evil day, and having done everything, to stand firm. Stand firm therefore, having girded your loins with truth, and having put on the breastplate of righteousness, and having shod your feet with the preparation of the gospel of peace; in addition to all, taking up the shield of faith with which you will be able to extinguish all the flaming missiles of the evil one. And take the helmet of salvation, and the sword of the Spirit, which is the word of God.

The Battle is Spiritual

In the first three chapters of Ephesians, Paul establishes the foundation for a new powerful identity through our relationship with Christ. In the final three chapters, he encourages us to begin living out, or putting into practice, our new identity. Paul closes the book of Ephesians with a rousing call to pick up and put on the protective armor of God.

Engaging the enemy is easier knowing that we are not desperately fighting *for* victory, because that has already been won at the Cross of Calvary. Rather, we are fighting the enemy *from* a position of victory. This changes our entire perspective on spiritual warfare!

We cannot physically sock Satan in the chops and begin a knock-down dragout because our battle is not against flesh and blood, as Paul states in 2 Corinthians 10:3-4:

For though we walk in the flesh, we do not war according to the flesh, for the weapons of our warfare are not of the flesh, but divinely powerful for the destruction of fortresses.

Since spiritual warfare is "spiritual," it must be fought on a spiritual level. The weapons we use must be spiritually effective if they are to do us any good. Realizing this very fact, God Himself provided armor which He knows to be "divinely powerful for the destruction of fortresses."

With this protective gear, we are able to "stand firm against the schemes of the devil." Though God has provided this armor for us, it is our responsibility to "take up" and "put on" that which He has furnished. He provides it and we are to utilize it. What good is armor if it sits at our feet and is never used? It is like a starving man sitting on a pile of food. He will continue to starve if he does not appropriate the abundance around him.

We desperately need every single piece of this armor. If any one piece is lacking, we are not fully protected. Imagine a front-line combat soldier with full battle gear, camouflaged suit, food pack, leather boots, and rifle, suddenly encountering the enemy. As the soldier points the rifle, aims his gun sights and shoots, nothing happens! He forgot to load his gun with bullets. Complete protection requires the "*full* armor of God."

The Belt of Truth

Paul lists six pieces of armor that help us withstand Satan. The order in which they appear in Ephesians 6 is the order in which a soldier would put them on. The first piece of armor to put on is the girdle of truth.

I was a bit taken back upon learning that I must wear a girdle, but once I grasped the meaning of doing so, I realized how essential it is to successful spiritual warfare.

In the days of the New Testament, a girdle was basically a belt. Before putting any other piece of equipment on, Roman soldiers would always tuck their tunic under a heavy leather belt so nothing would hinder them in any way from fighting effectively. To gird oneself was a mark of preparedness.

The equivalent counterpart for modern day believers is the belt of truth. That which holds together all other parts of our spiritual armor is truth. This truth involves two aspects which are important to us. First, we have come to know the truth. Jesus said, "I am the way, and the truth, and the life; no one comes to the Father, but through Me." We automatically came to the truth when we became a child of God. We left the lie of Satan and embraced the truth of Christ by meeting Him who is truth.

Second, girding our loins with truth also means implementing truth into practical, ordinary life situations. Because we have *come* to the truth, we can understand and walk *according* to the truth, through the help and power of the Holy Spirit who lives within. Choosing truth over Satan's lies becomes an everyday task.

Just as Roman soldiers tucked their tunic into their belt so the work of soldiering would be unimpeded, believers tuck away all distractions from battle so nothing interferes with their effectiveness to fight. Satan operates on lies and deceptive schemes, but we function on the basis of truth as found in Christ and His Word.

The Breastplate of Righteousness

The second piece of armor mentioned by Paul is the breastplate of righteousness. It was unthinkable for soldiers to enter into battle without this protective piece. The breastplate was sleeveless, covered the full torso, and was often made of leather or heavy linen. Sewn to this were overlapping slices of animal hooves, horns, or pieces of metal. Some were molded or hammered pieces of metal to form fit the body.

Preachers get extra mileage out of the breastplate illustration claiming that it only covered the front of a soldier and not the back. They make the point that we should face our enemy squarely because, if we run, our backs will not be protected. While that is a good illustration, it is not entirely correct as the soldier's breastplate often covered the back as well.

The purpose of the breastplate is to cover and protect vital organs such as the heart and lungs, as well as the intestines. In ancient Jewish thinking, the heart represented the mind and will, while the intestines represented the seat of our emotions. Satan fiercely attacks both of these areas.

The Christian's breastplate is identified as righteousness. It is the righteousness of Christ that protects our vital spiritual organs. As with truth, there are two aspects to our righteous breastplate. The first aspect refers to positional righteousness. The moment we came to Christ, we were justified and made righteous. The following verses point this out:

1 Corinthians 1:30

But by His doing you are in Christ Jesus, who became to us wisdom from God, and righteousness and sanctification, and redemption.

2 Corinthians 5:21

He made Him who knew no sin to be sin on our behalf, that we might become the righteousness of God in Him.

Philippians 3:8-9

More than that, I count all things to be loss in view of the surpassing value of knowing Christ Jesus my Lord, for whom I have suffered the loss of all things, and count them but rubbish in order that I may gain Christ, and may be found in Him, not having a righteousness of my own derived from the Law, but that which is through faith in Christ, the righteousness which comes from God on the basis of faith...

When Satan fires an accusing arrow our way saying, "You're not good enough to be a Christian," remind him of these Scriptural passages which firmly state our position before God.

Because we are positionally viewed as righteous does not mean that we can never engage in unrighteous deeds. We are saints who sometimes sin. The second aspect of the breastplate is actually living out, or putting into practice, the righteousness that is ours in Christ. Walking the path of holiness and godly living is a protective device against the enemy. While sin opens the door for demonic strongholds, righteousness slams the door shut.

Standing firm in our righteousness involves understanding and applying the principle of confession according to 1 John 1:9, "If we confess our sins, He is faithful and righteous to forgive us our sins and to cleanse us from all unrighteousness."

The word "confess" (homolegeo) literally means to acknowledge or to agree with something. Instead of ignoring sin, rationalizing it away, or indulging in it further, God desires that we agree with Him about the sin we commit. We can only work to correct the problem after we first agree that it is wrong.

Satan will make confession as difficult as he can for us. He wants us to believe that we have slid too far down the hill to ever get to the top again. He entices us to sin and then vehemently demeans us for doing it. Questioning our righteousness, our relationship with the Heavenly Father, and our ability to live holy lives, is all a part of his strategy.

While perfection awaits our future home in heaven, we can stand against the enemy by realizing our position of righteousness in Christ, by beginning to actually live out what God has declared us to be, and by preventing demonic strongholds in our life through daily confession of sin. As the old addage state, "An ounce of prevention is worth a pound of cure."

Righteousness cannot be lived out apart from confession. Confession of sin paves the way for a fruitful expression of righteousness in our daily living. Even Paul said in Acts 24:16, "I also do my best to maintain always a blameless conscience both before God and before men."

Shodding Our Feet With the Gospel

The third piece of armor mentioned in Ephesians 6 is the shoes of peace. To shod one's feet simply means to wear shoes. Continuing the imagery, shoes were important to Roman soldiers because they marched over all kinds of surfaces: rough hot roads, jagged rocks, thorns, wet stream beds, mud, mountains, etc. It is difficult to fight, let alone stand, with blistered, cut, swollen, or broken feet. Protective shoes precluded problems with the necessary movements of warfare such as running, fighting, or standing.

Many believe this piece of armor refers to our readiness to proclaim the gospel. They sense an allusion to Isaiah 52:7, "How lovely on the mountains are the feet of him who brings good news..." Paul even quotes this passage in Romans 10:17.

Just as a good pair of boots allowed soldiers to march, fight, or climb anywhere, followers of Christ are to "shod their feet with the preparation of the gospel of peace" by being ready to proclaim the gospel anywhere, at any time.

Because God is omniscient, He sees the entire picture of warfare. He knows the exact moment our neighbor will choose to follow Him and where we are most needed to proclaim His Word. We attack spiritual ground when our commander says, "Go here, and proclaim the good news!" and we immediately go.

While it is certainly true that believers should be prepared to obey the leading of the Lord at all times, the word "readiness" or "preparation" (hetoimos) can also refer to a prepared foundation or base. In other words, shoes furnish us with sure footing and a firm foundation from which to fight. Josephus described the shoes of a Roman soldier as "thickly studded with sharp nails." They were much like baseball cleats used to grip the ground for traction.

The "gospel of peace" refers to the good news that believers are at peace with God as Romans 5:1 declares, "Therefore, having been justified by faith, we have peace with God through our Lord Jesus Christ." We not only have peace *with* God, but we also have the peace *of* God. In John 14:7 Jesus says:

> *Peace I leave with you; My peace I give to you; not as the world gives, do I give to you. Let not your heart be troubled, nor let it be fearful.*

Because we have peace *with* God, Jesus gives us the peace *of* God. Philippians 4:7 clearly explains this benefit, "the peace of God, which surpasses all comprehension, shall guard your hearts and your minds in Christ Jesus." Colossians 3:15 even encourages us to let the peace of Christ rule in our hearts.

In essence, because we have made peace with God and Jesus gave us His peace, we can actually experience peace in this life and allow it to rule in our hearts. That peace acts as a cleated shoe in our spiritual life, helping us to stand firm against the devil. Satan promotes chaos and confusion to get our mind off of God, but Isaiah 26:3 (KJV) exhorts, "Thou wilt keep him in perfect peace whose mind is stayed on Thee; because he trusteth in Thee."

Satan has a difficult time with individuals who are at peace with God, themselves, and others, and who are experiencing the inner peace of the Lord on a daily basis. By understanding and implementing these aspects of peace, we dig our cleats into the ground, position ourselves securely, and find spiritual success.

The Shield of Faith

The fourth piece of armor mentioned by Paul is the shield of faith. Roman soldiers used several kinds of shields, but two were the most common. One was a small round shield about two feet in diameter secured to the soldier's arm by leather straps. It was lightweight and used to deflect the blows of an opponent's sword in hand-to-hand combat.

The other popular shield, and the one Paul refers to here, is the "thureos" shield. This shield measured 2 1/2 feet wide by 4 1/2 feet high and was designed to protect the entire body. It would be similar to carrying a small door in front of you. The protective benefits are obvious as flaming arrows either bounced off or struck the door instead of the soldier.

Contrary to popular perception, there is really nothing mysterious about faith. Biblical faith is simply what we believe about God and His Word. The more we know about God and His Word the greater our faith can be according to Romans 10:17 which states, "So faith comes from hearing, and hearing by the word of Christ."

The smaller our faith, the smaller our shield will be. Faith acts like a "thureos" shield. When Satan's flaming arrows assail us, we can stand behind our big thureos shield of faith. The more we learn and grow in our knowledge of God and His Word, the greater our faith will be.

The Helmet of Salvation

The fifth piece of armor involves the helmet of salvation. In Paul's day, soldiers wore helmets to protect themselves from the "rhomphaia" sword, a large double-edged sword measuring 3-4 feet in length. Swinging swords as they rode upon their horses, calvarymen tried to decapitate or split open the skulls of their opponents. Knowing there were fellas on horses indiscriminately swinging long, heavy, double-edged swords to cut your head off, ensuring that your helmet was on could mean the difference between life and death.

The head is essential because it directs the body. Our mind tells our body what to do, whether it is reaching for a glass of water or praying to the Lord. People sustaining head injuries often must learn how to walk, talk, and think again.

In a figurative sense, Satan likes to ride upon his horse indiscriminately swinging his large "rhomphaia" sword at the head of Christians. If he can mess up our thinking, he will mess up our behavior and steal glory away from God. This is why believing truth, living out truth, growing in truth, and filling our minds with truth is a protective helmet to the main control room of our lives.

The Sword of the Spirit

The sixth piece of armor supplied to believers is the sword of the Spirit. The sword Paul is referring to here is not the large "rhomphaia" sword, but a short two-edged cut and thrust sword measuring 6-18 inches long. It was the principal weapon in hand-to-hand combat.

The sword God has equipped us with is not a physical sword, but a spiritual sword. It is called the sword "of the Spirit" because Paul is referring to the nature of Scripture. God's word is spiritual. His sword is able to pierce the heart and accomplish spiritual tasks as described in Hebrews 4:12. It is "of the Spirit" because the Spirit of God empowers, directs, and applies it to each situation.

Scripture acts as both a defensive and offensive weapon.

Defensively, it deflects the blows of an opponent. As an offensive weapon, it is designed to cut precisely and quickly. This small sword reaches its full potential only when used skillfully.

The point is to use specific Scriptural truths to combat specific lies and attacks. If Satan tempts us with lust, quoting John 11:35 and saying "Jesus wept," will be of no help. We must use precise verses and specific teaching. When Jesus was tempted in the wilderness, He countered each temptation with a specific verse.

For instance, when Satan asserts that God is ashamed of us, we can quote Hebrews 2:11:

> *For both He who sanctifies and those who are sanctified are all from one Father, for which reason He is not ashamed to call them brethren.*

When he creates unfounded fear in ministry, we can quote 2 Timothy 1:7, "For God has not given us a spirit of timidity, but of power and love and discipline." The key to effectively using the sword of the Spirit with precision is knowing God's Word, studying it, memorizing it, and hiding it in our hearts.

Each piece of armor is part of God's divine outfit for us. They protect us from the enemy and help us defeat his vicious attacks. When properly outfitted, we become one "tough cookie" in the Lord. Putting on the armor, understanding the purpose and function of each piece, and actually using it, is of extreme necessity when battling Satan in spiritual warfare. A warrior without armor is like a field mouse without cover. The hawk easily sweeps down and carries it away. A proper understanding and utilization of our protective armor makes for mighty warriors.

Six

PRAYER, THE ULTIMATE WARFARE WEAPON

I doubt Satan feels too threatened by the kind of prayer occurring in the typical mid-week church service. As long as we are not binding him, releasing God's power against him, and reclaiming lost souls for Christ, Satan will let us be as religious as we wish. Warfare praying is front-line activity.

After reading about only six pieces of armor, you may be wondering if I have forgotten about prayer. But this significant aspect of the armor of God did not escape my notice. Devotion to prayer was not really part of the Roman soldier's outfit, but Paul adds it to the Christian warrior's gear because of its essential nature. As the ultimate warfare weapon, it must be included in the armor analogy.

After listing the six pieces of armor in Ephesians 6:10-17, the emphasis on prayer is slated in verses 18-20:

> *With all prayer and petition pray at all times in the Spirit, and with this in view, be on the alert with all perseverance and petition for all the saints, and pray on my behalf, that utterance may be given to me in the opening of my mouth, to make known with boldness the mystery of the gospel, for which I am an ambassador in chains; that in proclaiming it I may speak boldly, as I ought to speak.*

Paul exhorts believers to pray at all times "with all prayer and petition." Prayer is the Greek word "proseuche" and refers to general prayer requests, while petition "deesis" refers to very specific requests. Both general and specific prayers are needed in spiritual warfare. From personal experience, we know that some prayers are very general as we pray for "all the saints" and some are very directed as Paul specifically asked for enablement in sharing the gospel with clarity. Church evangelism teams usually offer general prayers before evangelism activities and upon returning, offer very specific prayers for the individuals with whom they shared.

In its simplest definition, prayer is communicating with God. Praying at all times, or being in constant communion with our Heavenly Father, is vital for a vibrant spiritual relationship. Through prayer, we express our dependence on God, seek His direction, and offer praise. He certainly knows our needs before we even ask, but He desires that we communicate those needs to Him through prayer.

The Christian life is a life of dependence. We are dependent upon God for our authority, our power, our new redeemed identity, our forgiveness of sins, and any spiritual impact we contribute. He is the vine and we are the branches. We are nothing without God.

In light of our humble dependence upon God, after putting on the armor, Paul instructs us to pray. 1 Peter 4:7 says, "Be of sound judgment and sober spirit for the purpose of prayer." If our mind becomes dull, we are less likely to act quickly and appropriately.

When the enemy tried to halt progress on repairing the walls of Jerusalem, Nehemiah and his followers defeated the enemy by watching *and* praying according to Nehemiah 4:9, "But we prayed to our God, and because of them we set up a guard against them day and night."

Dramatic Story of Prayer

The importance and impact of prayer is dramatically seen in the following missionary story. While on furlough at his home church in Michigan, a medical missionary told the following story:

> *While serving at a small field hospital in Africa, every two weeks I traveled by bicycle through the jungle to a nearby city for supplies. This was a journey of two days which required camping overnight at the halfway point. On one of these journeys, I arrived in the city where I planned to collect money from a bank, purchase medicine and supplies, and then begin my two-day journey back to the field hospi-*

tal. Upon arrival in the city I observed two men fighting, one of whom had been seriously injured. I treated him for his injuries, and at the same time witnessed to him of the Lord Jesus Christ. I then traveled two days, camping overnight, and arrived home without incident.

Two weeks later I repeated my journey. Upon arriving in the city, I was approached by the young man I had treated two weeks earlier. He told me that he had known that I carried money and medicines. He said, "Some friends and I followed you into the jungle, knowing that you would camp overnight. We were waiting just outside your campsite for you to go to sleep. We planned to kill you and take your money and drugs. But just as we were about to move into your campsite, we saw that you were surrounded by 26 armed guards."

At this, I laughed and said that I was certainly all alone out in that jungle campsite. The young man pressed the point, however, and said, "No, sir, I was not the only person to see the guards. My five friends also saw them, and we all counted them. It was because of those guards that we were afraid and left you alone."

At this point in the church presentation in Michigan, one of the men in the church jumped to his feet and interrupted the speaker. He asked, "Sir, can you tell me the exact day that this incident happened?" It took the missionary a moment to recall, but he could. When he informed the congregation of the date, the man who had interrupted him told his story...

"When it is night in Africa, it is day here. On the night of your incident in Africa, it was morning here, and I was preparing to go play a game of golf. As I was putting my golf bag in the car, I felt the Lord leading me to pray for you. In fact, the urging of the Lord was so strong that I called the men in this church together to meet with me here in the sanctuary and pray for you. Would all of those men with me on that day, please stand up?" The men who met together to pray that day stood.

When all were counted, the number was 26. This is the power of prayer that overcomes the dark deeds of the enemy.[6]

Talking or Praying?

A survey I once read indicated that pastors spend less than five minutes a day in prayer. If this is true of pastors, how much less time is devoted to prayer for the average parishioner? Although severely diminished in our day, prayer is where the action is.

Any church without an undergirding of vibrant prayer is simply coasting on empty. The church's prayer movement must be based on a correct worldview. Any worldview, other than a biblical one, minimizes the impact and effectiveness of prayer and shortchanges the experience for the person praying.

We often spend more time talking *about* prayer and the prayer meeting itself than we do actually praying. It is far easier to theologically agree that prayer is a doctrinally correct thing to do, than it is to actually get around to the task of praying.

If my pastoral experience represents the norm, then the typical Wednesday night Bible study and prayer time is falling far short of its worthy intention. The meeting usually involves announcements, the mention of special prayer requests, and a one-half hour Bible study that is usually prolonged because of comments, questions, and opinions. Prayer is squeezed out and the pressure is on to hurry up and finish because the clock is striking eight o'clock and the children's programs are over.

Often prayer needs are passed out on sheets of paper. Upon breaking into smaller groups for prayer, sometimes there is more talking and visiting going on than there is praying. People have their pens handy checking off each request as it is prayed for and when the list is done, they are done. After all, they did finish the list. They then sit around and visit some more.

Something is missing in this scenario. Prayer seems more mechanical and less inspired by the Holy Spirit. Many people come on Wednesday out of a devotion to church attendance rather than a devotion to communicate with the living God. Prayer then, becomes lifeless. It is wasted breath that makes us feel good about ourselves for having attended yet another church function, but nothing powerful is accomplished. Too often we pray for insignificant items like the corn growing on Margaret's big toe, instead of using prayer as a weapon to destroy Satanic strongholds.

In one particular church, the leadership wanted to emphasize more prayer. To set the stage, they allowed 15 minutes of worship in song while leaving a full 45-50 minutes for the essential task of praying. It did not work. Why? Because people did not know how to pray! After going through their list in 8-12 minutes, they did not know what to do with themselves. Binding the strong man is a warfare activity which takes a great deal of effort.

In contrast, another church I pastored did this very well. It was a smaller church, but we prayed solidly for 45-60 minutes without even a prayer list. It was wonderful being led by the Spirit, opening oneself up to God, and expressing complete dependence upon Him.

Is prayer a vital part of your personal life? Do you spend more time talking *about* prayer than you do actually praying? Is prayer a dynamic aspect of your local church or are you routinely going through motions filled with emptiness? These are important questions because the victory we experience as followers of Christ is directly proportionate to the quality of our prayer life.

Front-line Warfare

Prayer is often viewed as a spiritual support activity bringing up the rear of an advancing army, securely tucked away from any real danger. This, however, is a fallacious view of prayer.

Far from being a support activity, prayer *is* the actual front line of spiritual warfare. It is not an option, but an essential, vital ingredient for success. Prayer is not merely a weapon to be used, it is the very heart of the battle. This is why warfare praying is so difficult for most of us. Spiritual warfare without prayer is like Raisin Bran without raisins. The two are intricately linked together.

A colleague of mine began to pray specifically against Satanic strongholds in every country. He literally took a map and prayed an hour a day for these countries. The opposition to such praying was so harsh that he has since given it up. Who knows what great things God could have accomplished through his prayers? This episode does, however, relay a truth. Satan harassed this man severely because he was working the front lines. We expect to be shot at when working the front line of the battle. Prayer, real prayer, is the ultimate spiritual warfare weapon.

Is our lackadaisical approach to prayer due to a deficient view of God? Is God no longer seen as the great emancipator of souls who releases sinners from the bondage of sin? Has He become our heavenly slot machine where we put in a few nickels of praise and a couple quarters of religious jargon and out pops the answer to our prayer request?

Has our vision of God's supreme ability grown dim and our expectations of Him fallen to new lows? Listen to your prayers and the prayers of your church, and see for yourself if the majority of prayers fall on a level far below what God is able to do and what God desires to do.

Spiritual warfare involves a theology that God is big enough to accomplish anything. Pray for big things expecting God to do a wondrous work. Pray for entire nations, entire cities, and entire neighborhoods. Our God is remarkably able to meet the requests of His children who pray believing that He will answer. Pray with vision and great expectation as John Knox prayed, "Give me Scotland or I die!"

Prayers of Praise and Adoration

Warfare praying is not only praying *against* something, or asking *for* something, it can also be a time of *affirming* the sovereignty and holiness of God, His everlasting love, and the victory and benefits of Calvary.

Including praise and adoration in prayer bolsters our faith because we are focusing on the character, nature, and attributes of our Heavenly Father. Faith is simply what we believe about God. It becomes stronger as we affirm in our hearts who He is and what He is able to accomplish. Additionally, by including praise and adoration in our prayers, we glorify God and accomplish the very thing Satan seeks to nullify. Prayer that exalts God and ascribes glory to His name derails Satan's pernicious plans.

Doctrinal Prayers

In addition to praising God, praying with a warfare mentality also involves doctrinal prayers. Because the groundwork for Satan's predictable and customary method of operating is deception and lies, one of the ways to overcome him is embracing and believing the truth. When truth exposes his lies, strongholds are diminished. Praying the truth of God's Word not only reinforces our faith, it exposes Satan's lies by applying specific passages of Scripture to specific situations.

A sample prayer rich in doctrine might look this:

> *Gracious Heavenly Father. I desire to draw near Your throne of grace with boldness and confidence knowing that You are ready to provide help, grace, and mercy in my time of need. This privilege is not anything I have gained on my own merit, but a privilege You have given to me as Your child. You are the vine and I am the branch. All that I am and all that I possess come because I am connected to and dependent upon the vine. I come before You out of obedience to Your Word and on the basis of the holiness and righteousness that is mine through Jesus Christ. According to Your Word I desire to pray only according to Your will and believe that the Holy Spirit will intercede for me during this time.*
>
> *I offer you a sacrifice of praise from my lips for who You are and what You do. I stand united in victory with my Savior Jesus Christ. I stand in the truth that I am a child of God, born from above, and a joint heir of Jesus Christ. Even*

though I am an alien and stranger on this earth, I thank You that my true citizenship is in heaven and that I have been seated with You in the heavenlies. Father, accept my praise and adoration for the victory You won at Calvary. I thank You that Jesus experienced the same temptations I face yet, He was without sin and defeated Satan's deceptive attacks. Thank You for the assurance that I too can experience victory over the enemy by appropriating Your victory at Calvary as my own.

I praise You for the crucifixion and resurrection of my Lord Jesus Christ. I affirm that Your work on the cross defeated Satan and that through the shed blood of Jesus Christ I find freedom from the bondage of sin. Thank You that I am a new creature in Christ created for good works. I desire to live according to my new nature. Help me to bring glory and honor to Your name through my thoughts and actions. In accordance with Your Word, I yield the members of my body to the control and influence of the Holy Spirit. Direct and guide me as I desire to walk according to the Spirit of God. Fill me with Your Spirit and help me be sensitive to His leading as I walk in faith according to my new identity in Christ. Help me realize and recognize that You have provided me with everything needed for a life which brings glory and honor to Your name.

Heavenly Father, I claim my position of authority and victory over Satan and his cohorts. I affirm that You raised Jesus from the dead and seated Him on a throne of power far above all principalities and powers and that I am seated there with Him. I take up and put on the full armor of God as I walk on this earth. Help me discern the deceptive schemes of the enemy. Thank You for watching over me and caring for me as a shepherd cares for his sheep. I love You God with all of my being and only desire to please You. In the name of Jesus Christ I pray. Amen.

Although this prayer is very broad in nature, it is rich in doctrine. Many of the themes and much of the wording is straight from Scripture. Doctrinal prayers can be very specific. For instance, if Satan brings confusion about your identity in Christ, pray the truths of Scripture which affirm the truth of this area. If Satan creates confusion surrounding the assurance of your salvation, pray the truths of Scripture which affirm this area. If Satan claims he has a right to invade and harass certain areas of your life, pray the truth of Scripture regarding these areas.

The entire point is to expose and confront Satan's lie with the powerful truth of God's Word which acts like a giant spotlight illuminating the dark shadows where Satan hides. You will be pleasantly surprised at how much you enjoy praying doctrinally and how much it helps you believe and affirm God's Word. It is a communion experience with God, a great way to learn truth, and at the same time, a method of spiritual warfare against Satan.

Evangelistic Praying

According to 2 Corinthians 4:3-4, Satan blinds the minds of unbelievers to the truth:

> *And even if our gospel is veiled, it is veiled to those who are perishing, in whose case the god of this world has blinded the minds of the unbelieving, that they might not see the light of the gospel of the glory of Christ, who is the image of God.*

Unless their eyes are open to the need for a Savior, people cannot come to Christ. Since Satan blinds them from seeing and realizing the truth, we attack in prayer to remove that blindness. Even Jesus taught that we cannot plunder a strong man's house unless we first bind the strong man (Mt. 12:29).

If thieves broke into our house, they would have a much easier time stealing our television set, silverware, etc., if they first tied us to a chair, disabling us from interfering with their actions. In a similar way, binding Satan restrains his action or behavior against someone or something so he is unable to interfere with our evangelistic efforts. It is entirely appropriate to use prayer for combatting spiritual blindness caused by Satan. When entering enemy territory, prayer must lead the way.

The target of our prayer is the binding and restraining of the strong man. Satan's power was broken at the Cross, but he will not let go of anything he thinks he can keep until we exercise the authority delegated to us by the Lord Jesus Christ. Using prayer as an evangelistic tool brings light to darkness, sight to blindness, and spiritual truth to deceptive lies.

Not only is prayer used offensively as an evangelistic tool, but as a defensive weapon, a prayer for "opening eyes" can also be used for believers as demonstrated by Paul in Ephesians 1:18-19. Here he prays that the eyes of believers may be enlightened to fully understand the spiritual power, authority, and protection which is theirs in Christ.

The truth of 1 John 15:14-15 also encourages us to pray:

> *And this is the confidence which we have before Him, that, if we ask anything according to His will, He hears us. And if we know that He hears us in whatever we ask, we know that we have the requests which we have asked from Him.*

Persistence in Praying

Lest we think warfare praying is as easy as pushing the buttons on our remote control, it often involves determined persistence as demonstrated in the story of the widow who took her case against an adversary to a judge. Knowing she was on the right side of the law, she demanded justice. Her persistence was rewarded as she was finally granted her request (Lk. 18:1-8).

The purpose of the story is declared in the first verse, "Now He was telling them a parable to show that at all times they ought to pray and not to lose heart." In dealing with our adversary, persistence is necessary. Prevailing prayer is persistent faith which finds

God's will and insists on it against the enemy.

The Old Testament parallel for persistent praying may be found in the book of Daniel. When the angel came with the answer to Daniel's prayer in Daniel 10:12-13, he said:

> *Do not be afraid, Daniel, for from the first day that you set your heart on understanding this and on humbling yourself before your God, your words were heard, and I have come in response to your words. But the prince of the kingdom of Persia was withstanding me for twenty-one days; then behold, Michael, one of the chief princes, came to help me, for I had been left there with the kings of Persia.*

The first time Daniel prayed, God began to immediately send the answer. The delay was caused by warfare in the spiritual realm. Daniel's persistent faith and prevailing prayer led him to fast and pray for twenty-one days. Front-line warfare praying involves the same kind of persistence seen in Daniel's prayer and the widow's story. Persistence sees the will of God accomplished.

Prayer is not merely a friendly chat with the Savior for a few minutes each day. A correct perspective on prayer includes the kind of praying that releases God's power against the enemy, binds the strong man, then plunders and reclaims lost territory.

It takes time, effort, and discipline to pray. *It is work.* But the effort is certainly worthwhile because we know that prayer is effective. *Prayer works.* James 5:16 states, "The effective prayer of a righteous man can accomplish much."

Specific Suggestions

In his book *Demon Possession and the Christian,* Fred Dickason provides several specific suggestions on how to pray for someone harassed by demons:[7]

> *1. Pray that the demons may be cut off from all communication and help from other demons and Satan.*

2. Pray that the demons would be confused and weakened in their hold on the person.

3. Pray that counselees would be strengthened in their faith to understand their position in Christ and to trust and obey God's Word.

4. Pray that the person may be able to distinguish between his thoughts and feelings, and those of Satan.

5. Pray that the person might recognize the demonic presence and not be confused, but willingly seek godly counsel and help.

6. Pray that God would protect and guide His child and set angelic forces at work to break up every scheme of the enemy.

I doubt that Satan feels too threatened by the kind of prayer occurring in the typical mid-week church service. As long as we are not binding him, releasing God's power against him, and reclaiming lost souls for Christ, Satan will let us be as religious as we wish. Warfare praying is front-line activity. Although Satan will not appreciate our serious efforts at prayer, the Kingdom of God will not be advanced if the front line is unsecured and unattended.

Prayer is war! Sitting on the fence post is an impossibility for Christians. By virtue of our identity as a child of God, we have already declared our allegiance with Christ and are already involved in the battle. We may be winning or we may be losing the battle, but there is no neutrality. Hopefully, this book will help you win more often and lose less frequently.

Warfare is difficult and unpleasant at times, but until we reach our final eternal destination in the very presence of God, we fight in the ongoing battles. Prayer is a necessary, strategic, and effective front-line weapon employed against our adversary. I encourage you to raise prayer above the typical mundane experience and lift it to new heights of effectiveness through warfare praying.

This involves strategically praying prayers of praise and adoration, believing God for greater victory, praying the truth of Scripture, binding the strong man, and praying to remove spiritual blindness. This perspective of prayer enables us to become significant contributors in the Kingdom of God. Since the final outcome of the war is never in doubt, we can utilize our delegated authority and our spiritual armor to attack the enemy with great fervor.

SEVEN

POWER, TRUTH AND AUTHORITY

It is unnecessary to pray for what we already have. There is no need to ask for the equipment and authority needed to defeat our enemy because God has already given it to us. It is like the man looking for his glasses when all along they are on top of his head.

There are two main methods for loosening Satan's grip in a person's life. The first method is called a power encounter. Its greatest support is found in the Gospels where Jesus used His power to cast out demons. He then delegated this authority to His disciples who gloated over the fact that even the demons were subject to their authority (Mt. 10:1-15; Mk. 6:7-13; Lk. 9:1-6; 10:17-22). Jesus would later give that same authority to every single believer (Mt. 28:18-20).

In a power encounter, the power of Satan and his demons oppose a greater power, God and His angels. When the two clash in warfare, one will win the battle and one will lose. Since God is the greater power, He will win if believers exercise faith.

Extreme advocates of this position believe that power encounters are necessary for the evangelism and growth of the church. When people see the working of miracles, that is, casting out demons or a display of powerful acts, they will more likely believe.

Biblical examples of this occur in such passages as Acts 5:12-14 and 8:4-8. Acts 5 indicates that because of the numerous signs and wonders occurring through the Apostles, many believed. Acts 8 delineates that many became believers because of the signs Philip performed while in Samaria.

However, there are also examples of miracles occurring where no belief follows, as in John 6:36; 7:5; Acts 14:8ff; 16:16-24. Jesus often did not fare well in the eyes of some observers despite His miracles. Many became more rigid in their unbelief.

In response to those who followed Him for all the wrong reasons, Jesus states in John 6:36, "You have seen Me, and yet do not believe." John 7:5 reveals that, "not even His brothers were believing in Him." In a similar vein, the Apostle Paul endured tremendous suffering at the hands of those who saw the signs and wonders that he performed. They hardened their hearts, instead of believing upon the Savior which Paul so eloquently spoke.

While power encounters may be a useful evangelism tool, it seems that an overt miracle, or casting out of demons, is not *necessary* for individuals to believe, nor did belief *always* occur when these powers were displayed. There will always be those who reject the truth regardless of how it is presented. The fact remains that Jesus cast out demons and healed people anyway, and He commanded His followers to do the same.

The Truth Encounter

The truth encounter method stresses the content of the Epistles over the content of the Gospels. The claim is made that power encounter events in the Gospels occurred *before* the Cross and therefore do not apply to believers today, because we live in the dispensation *after* the Cross. The Epistles are our main manual now, not the Gospels. The Epistles speak of truth over falsehood, not the casting out of demons.

This view focuses on truth, not power. Without truth, demons may return and make things worse than before (Mt. 12:43-45). The strategy is not to "out-power" Satan, but to "out-truth" him through proclaiming and acting upon Scripture, God's truth.

Because he is a deceiver, Satan conducts his operations in a covert fashion. To expose his undercover operation, one utilizes the truth of God. Satan's power is in his deceptive lies. If he cannot deceive us, then he has no power over us. The truth of God's Word brings light to the darkness, truth to the lie, and freedom to the bondage of deception.

An experience from my days as a young paper boy helps to illustrate this point. It was always difficult to deliver the paper to a certain house because of a vicious little dog. I allowed this little runt to keep me in a state of fear, preventing me from delivering the paper to its proper place. It was my belief that if I got too close or he ever got loose, he would rip my head off. The only power the little dog had over me was the power I attributed to him. In other words, my belief, which happened to be totally incorrect, controlled my behavior.

Had I known then what I know now, I would have confronted that little high-pitched bark of his. His seemingly ferocious bark would have turned into a whinny yelp as he tucked his tail between his legs running for cover.

Satan is like that little dog. If we believe he can rip our heads off, we will be paralyzed with fear, unable to act as victorious children of God. However, believing and utilizing the truth of God's Word helps us expose the devil's deceptive lies and see him for what he is, a tiny Yorkshire Terrier trying to act like a Great Dane.

A Both/And Proposition

Which model is right? Should we forget about one in favor of the other? May I suggest that it need not be an *either/or* situation? It can be, and should be, a *both/and* proposition. The best method actually makes use of both power and truth. In other words, utilize the truth model, but be prepared to exercise power and authority when necessary.

In my own experience with oppressed individuals, I have seen great success in exposing Satan's deceptive lie and bringing God's truth to fruition. Yet, even as I bring God's truth into the demonic equation, I have sensed great power struggles in the making.

For instance, during my sessions with oppressed individuals, Satan has brought about mental confusion and fear that he will harm them or a family member if they continue. He has even brought on physical problems such as difficulty with breathing.

Since my strategy is to help the individual affirm and apply the truth of God for himself/herself, I simply cannot allow demons to interfere with the process. I have to exert my delegated power and authority in Christ to stop their negative involvement. Binding demons, not allowing them to call up reinforcements, demanding that they submit to the authority of Christ, and commanding them to be quiet and restrain from interfering with the thought processes of the individual, are a few of the power tactics utilized. In my experience, power encounter and truth encounter go hand in hand and when used together make an unstoppable team.

Yelling at the top of my lungs and prancing about like a lunatic are not the tactics I employ. Authority does not come through the decibel level of one's voice, but rather through a firm inner confidence in Christ and a strong belief in the power of Scripture.

Afflicted individuals should take an active role in this process, for if the demon tries to come back, they can resist him for themselves rather than relying upon the deliverance team every time they encounter spiritual warfare. Truth and power are two sides of the same coin which make the Christian an unconquerable foe.

The Believer's Authority

Advertisements placed in weight lifting magazines often show the boys of muscle walking off with beautiful ladies after ridiculing a frail man. The implication is that weak men lose out. In the next frame, however, after using certain protein products, the weak man becomes strong and muscular, beats up on the boys of muscle who once mocked him, and walks away with the beautiful ladies.

Satan, like the boys of muscle, picks on spiritual weaklings and walks off in triumph. If we are going to stand up to Satan and his henchmen, we must have the authority and strength to do so. If we had no authority, we would be mere mice attempting to fight a cat, a battle not likely to be won. When we realize that we are strong and that our authority stems from the authority of Christ, then our spiritual weakness turns into unconquerable boldness. We spiritually beat up the boys of Satan who once mocked us, and walk away with the victory!

Does a Christian really have any right to exercise spiritual authority over demons? When Jesus commissioned the seventy in Luke 10, He clearly gave them the right to use His authority.

In the Great Commission of Matthew 28:18-20, which of course applies to all believers, Jesus makes it clear that He calls us and sends us under His authority. Those who go and make disciples operate with delegated authority over Satan and demons. Since the Great Commission applies to each believer, every Christian has this delegated authority.

The prevalent "me-first mindset" and the cry for individual rights which is so evident in our culture, weakens our concept of authority. By combining our culture's questioning of authority with a lack of real belief in Satan and demons, it is easy to understand why Christians are unprepared to repel enemy attacks, and invade and plunder rebel territory with confidence, authority, and victory.

Too often when we encounter satanic oppression, we scurry to the Lord like whipped puppies asking Him to take care of the big bully who made us run scared. God is likely to say, "My delegated authority is already at your disposal. Use what I have given you and take care of the bully yourself."

It is unnecessary to pray for what we already have. There is no need to ask for the equipment and authority needed to defeat our enemy because God has already given it to us. It is like the man looking for his glasses when all along they are on top of his head.

Jude 9 specifically states that not even Michael, the archangel, dared to pronounce a judgment against Satan but said, "The Lord rebuke you." Should we exercise authority over demons when Michael would not even use authority against Satan?

The question is a proper one, but two items must be considered. First, Jesus Himself commanded us to go and make disciples in Matthew 28:18-20. This implies that delegated authority is needed to fulfill His commission. Yes, we should utilize our authority.

Second, a consideration of the context of Jude reveals the problem to be men who "reject authority and revile angelic majesties" according to verse 8. In other words, they reject the concept of living under God's authority and act upon their own assumed authority. Apart from Christ, we have absolutely no basis for authority over demons. However, if we are the ambassadors of Him who possesses ultimate power over demons, and He has delegated His authority to us, then we have the right to utilize it, and are even expected to do so.

The Policeman Analogy

In his book entitled *The Authority of the Believer*, John MacMillan illustrates the concept of authority by comparing it to the authority of a policeman.[8] If a stranger knocks on our door and asks to search our house, we would not allow it because we are under no obligation to let him enter. However, if the man is wearing a police uniform, identifies himself as a police officer, wears a badge, and presents a search warrant, we would allow him to conduct his business.

These two individuals are treated differently because one possesses no authority whatsoever, while the other works for the state and has been given the authority to search the house. As a representative of the government, his badge, uniform, and search warrant, represent authority delegated to him by the state.

It cannot be stated strongly enough that the authority we possess over demons is delegated authority. In and of ourselves, apart from Christ, we are utterly powerless against the devil's schemes. James 4:7 reveals that we are to resist the devil, but only after we have submitted to God. Our authority comes from our relationship with a God who is all powerful.

It matters very little whether the police officer is a twenty year veteran or a rookie cop. The badge they both wear is backed by the same authority. The veteran may have more wisdom, tact, and skill in utilizing his authority, but it is nonetheless the same authority. In Luke 10, the seventy reported back that they had cast out demons, even though it was their first ministry experience.

Placing authority in the hands of human beings does have its dangers. Satan will use our success to tempt us toward independence from God, a wise move on his part. But according to Philippians 3:3, we are to "glory in Christ Jesus and put no confidence in the flesh." Since the weapons of our warfare are not of the flesh (2 Cor. 10:4), resorting to our own personal strength is futile.

No matter what the subject, if we are successful with it, we tend to turn that success into a formula. Formula mentality believes that if the right words are said, Jesus' name is spoken, the hand is placed on the forehead, etc., then success is guaranteed. If we pop a coin into the machine, punch the right combination of buttons, out comes victory.

This belittles God and misses out on the main point behind the power we possess. Authority does not reside in formulas, saying exactly the right words, merely speaking the name of Jesus, or placing our hand in the right spot on the forehead. The seven sons of Sceva found this out in Acts 19. They soon realized that Paul's authority was not the result of a memorized formula or simply saying the name of Jesus. Paul's authority arose from his personal relationship with God.

Jesus even said in Matthew 7:22-23:

> *Many will say to Me on that day, Lord, Lord, did we not prophesy in Your name, and in Your name cast out demons, and in Your name perform many miracles? And then I will declare to them, I never knew you; depart from Me, you who practice lawlessness.*

Many deeds will be done in Christ's name, but it will be of little eternal value if there is no personal relationship with the Lord.

We will not experience effective authority over demons if we are not living under the authority of Christ. Living in sin during the week and trying to utilize God's delegated authority on the weekends is a recipe for failure and frustration. Living in humble submission to God is expected and necessary for successful spiritual warfare (1 Pet. 5:6-10).

Is God's Power Sufficient?

Although we would never publicly admit it, there may be internal doubt regarding God's ability to sustain us. The last thing we want is to engage the enemy if there is a possibility that our firepower is deficient. We do not want to fail.

Ephesians 1:18-23 addresses this very issue:

> *I pray that the eyes of your heart may be enlightened, so that you may know what is the hope of His calling, what are the riches of the glory of His inheritance in the saints, and what is the surpassing greatness of His power toward us who believe. These are in accordance with the working of the strength of His might which He brought about in Christ, when He raised Him from the dead, and seated him at His right hand in the heavenly places, far above all rule and authority and power and dominion, and every name that is named, not only in this age, but also in the one to come. And He put all things in subjection under His feet, and gave Him as head over all things to the church, which is his body, the fullness of Him who fills all in all.*

We can rest assured that the same power which sustains us is the same power that resurrected Jesus from the dead and seated Him in a place of honor, power, and authority, far above *all* rule and authority both in this age and in the one to come. The head of the church, the One commanding us to invade Satan's territory and reclaim lost souls, is none other than the head of the entire universe! The source and ability of the power that sustains us is not in question and deserves our full confidence.

Although we are physically living on Earth, our spiritual status finds us seated with Christ in the heavenlies. Successful spiritual warfare is possible because of our connection with Him.

Christ not only delegated to us the authority needed to *confront* the rebel prince, He also gave us the power *over* demons. Good management strategy never delegates responsibility without the accompanying resources to get the job done. Jesus commissioned us and also gave us authority to accomplish the task.

Ingredients For Success

Proficiently exercising authority over demons involves several essential ingredients which provide a sure foundation for success.

The first essential ingredient is faith. As stated previously, faith simply means "belief." It is what we believe to be true. How will we find success over demons if we do not believe we have authority over them? If our belief is weak, then our expression of that belief will also be weak and ineffective. But if we confidently grasp Christ's delegated authority, we will exercise it in a powerful way.

The second essential ingredient is a proper perspective of both God and ourselves. The right perspective properly places our confidence in God and not in ourselves. John 15:5 states, "I am the vine you are the branches; he who abides in Me and I in him, he bears much fruit; for apart from Me you can do nothing." Pride says, "I did it all by myself," but humility says, "Christ did it through me." Christ's work is accomplished through us because, as branches, we are connected to the vine.

The third essential ingredient is courage. Spiritual warfare demands that we be strong in the Lord, ready to move with boldness and bravery. The night before Joshua was to conquer the promised land, he was encouraged four times to be strong and courageous in the Lord (Josh. 1: 6,7,9,18). In considering their mission to proclaim the Word of God in Jerusalem, the Early Church prayed for and received boldness, according to Acts 4:29,31.

Many Christians fear Satan. They do not want to think about him, talk about him, pray against him, or encounter him in any way. Any involvement is far too risky. They fail to realize that they are already involved with Satan because of their relationship with Christ. If we cower in fear on the sidelines refusing to enter the battle, all the armor in the world will not help us.

Revelation 21:6-8 reveals that cowards will be lined up at the lake of fire alongside murderers, immoral persons, sorcerers and idolaters, and liars. This is a good reminder to heed 2 Timothy 1:7, "For God has not given us a spirit of timidity, but of power and love and discipline."

Satan wants us to fear him, his power, and his actions. Maintaining a healthy respect for our enemy is fine, but in light of our responsibility and accompanying authority, there is no reason for fear to paralyze us from action.

Spiritual warfare involves faith, a proper perspective, and bold courage. When these ingredients are mixed together with our Lord's commission and our accompanying authority, Satan cannot stand in our way.

EIGHT

STEPS TO FREEDOM

Demons are like rigid strands of spaghetti which become limp when soaked in water. They may stand firm at first, but they soon weaken when confronted with the powerful truth of God.

While teaching this material to college and seminary students, numerous individuals have contacted me long after the class was over saying, "I did not think a course on spiritual warfare would be of much benefit to me, but now I can't see how I ever managed without it. It was one of the most important courses I have ever enrolled in." It is one thing to preach *about* Satan from the pulpit, but quite another thing to *know what to do* when someone is experiencing demonic harassment.

The Right Methodology

While there is no rigid three-step formula which automatically causes demons to leave, there are specific elements that should be a part of every methodology. We do not want to promote a formulaic response, but we do want to ensure that important elements are not left out of the process.

The five-step deliverance method outlined in this book should not be taken as *the* definitive process and is certainly not an exhaustive response to the subject. However, it incorporates the basic and necessary ingredients for success in a deliverance ministry.

During my early experiences with this type of ministry, I constantly wondered if I was adhering to the right procedure and if all the necessary steps were done in the right order. I began thinking more about correct procedure than about setting an individual free.

This simple five-step outline has been developed for use in

deliverance situations. Although these five steps are broad and comprehensive in scope, it stands to reason that once they are learned, the specific items under each category will more easily come to mind. Because of varying theological perspectives, particular needs, and personal experiences, you may wish to tailor the specific instructions under each of these broad categories:

Five Point Deliverance Outline

1. Personal Preparation
2. Gathering Information
3. Setting the Tone
4. Dealing with Truth and Sin Issues
5. Post-deliverance Care

1. PERSONAL PREPARATION

Obviously, this is the first step with almost anything we do. When we must confront a brother involved in sin, Galatians 6:1 exhorts us to "restore such a one in a spirit of gentleness; each one looking to yourself, lest you too be tempted." Jesus even asks us to take the log out of our own eye before taking the speck out of our brother's eye (Mt. 7:1-5). Before celebrating the Lord's Supper, we are first asked to examine ourselves (1 Cor. 10:28). A time of personal preparation was included in many of the Old Testament festivals. The theme of self-examination is woven into the fabric of Scripture and functions with the dual purpose of both preparing and protecting us.

Since spiritual warfare is exactly what it states, warfare, it is of the utmost importance that we are prepared for battle. During this time of personal preparation we are asking, "Am I ready for what is about to occur?" In answering this question, it is helpful to explore several different areas of our life.

Prayer

The first and most significant area of readiness involves prayer, the defensive and offensive front line. This is an appropriate time to seek the Lord's wisdom and discernment for handling the situation. After all, James 1:5 encourages us to do this, "But if any of you lacks wisdom, let him ask of God, who gives to all men generously and without reproach, and it will be given to him."

In prayer we commit ourselves to Him and ask to be filled and controlled by the influence of the Holy Spirit. Spending time praising the Lord and ascribing honor and glory to His holy name is a fruitful preparatory event. Prior to engaging the enemy, it is essential that we spend time communicating with the Lord in prayer.

A Proper Perspective

A proper perspective is the second area for self-examination. An accurate outlook views deliverance as God's battle to be fought, not a personal flesh and blood war. It is God's power and God's truth that will prevail, not the power of a human being.

In other words, we maintain balance instead of over-rating ourselves or under-rating God. It is appropriate to keep in mind our position and authority in Christ, the victory that is ours because of Calvary, and the defeated status of our enemy. Because we minister in the strength of the Lord, our perspective must be biblically balanced, for Satan will surely take advantage of a lofty view of ourselves or a lowly view of God.

Putting on the Armor of God

Verbally putting on each piece of the armor of God, as found in Ephesians 6, is the third area of personal preparation. Verbally affirming the power of each piece of armor and its valuable protection in our lives ensures that we do not forget one of them.

For instance, in putting on the sword of the Spirit we might say:

> *And now Father, I take up and put on the sword of the Spirit as You instructed me to do in Ephesians 6:17. I wear it by faith and appropriate it unto myself by faith. Thank You for providing me with the weapon of Your holy Word which is sharp and powerful as a two-edged sword, able to pierce between soul and spirit, joints and marrow, and the*

thoughts and intentions of the heart. As Jesus used Scripture to defeat the enemy, enable me to do the same. Bring to memory specific verses as needed and help me to use Your Word in a wise and timely fashion. Amen.

Outside Prayer Support

The fourth item considered for self-examination is outside prayer support. Enlisting the prayer assistance of others familiar with spiritual warfare tactics fortifies the entire operation. When the enemy tests the front line, he will find it to be sturdy and filled with reinforcements.

Since church prayer chains are often nothing more than a gossip line, be sure to enlist serious prayer warriors who understand their role and function. Choose individuals who desire to open their lips to God instead of gossiping to one another. There is no need to divulge confidential information, but do provide your prayer support team with as much information as discretion allows so they can pray specifically and appropriately. The increased prayer support can be an essential ingredient for victory.

While working with a demonically oppressed individual, I came to an impasse. It felt like I could only go so far before running into a brick wall. Realizing my dilemma, I quickly made several phone calls and asked specific individuals to immediately begin praying. With the increased prayer support, I was able to successfully complete the process and help the counselee find freedom from demonic harassment. The increased prayer support was the difference between being stuck, and moving on. In hindsight, it would have been far wiser for me to enlist the needed prayer support prior to the battle, rather than in the midst of it.

Sweet Communion With God

Maintaining a dynamic relationship of sweet communion with the Lord is the fifth foundational item necessary for personal preparation. Incongruity between what we say and what we do leads to failure. It simply means to "let your walk match your talk."

A personal inventory of our relationship with God may reveal specific areas in our life where repentance and confession are necessary. The Holy Spirit will lead us into all truth, even the truth about ourselves. His loving searchlight is a powerful tool for exposing any kinks in our armor.

The last thing we want is for Satan to puff up his chest and accuse us of sin in our own life. Personal holiness forms a protective hedge around his accusations. They fall on deaf ears when we ensure that nothing is hindering our sweet communion with Him.

Meditate Upon God's Word

As part of a personal inventory, I have found it profitable to meditate upon God and His truth. By this, I mean consciously thinking about God's power, glory, authority, love, etc. I meditate upon specific passages of Scripture and important truths I must be grounded in prior to engaging the enemy. This helps set my mind on God's ability and His desire to set individuals free.

Any prized athlete worth his salt takes time before the big event to mentally and physically prepare himself for what is to come. In like manner, believers involved in deliverance ministries must also prepare themselves for the counseling session. A lack of personal preparation can hinder our effectiveness to the detriment of the counselee. Taken seriously, self-examination is a vital first step when engaging the enemy.

2. GATHERING INFORMATION

The second step in the five-point outline involves the gathering of pertinent information from the counselee prior to proceeding with deliverance. This process not only arms us with the knowledge of problematic areas in need of attention, but the insight gained forms the basis for devising a mental plan of action. Since Satan walks into a believer's life through open doors, gathering information helps us discover which doors are open so we can slam them shut. Vital information from the counselee assists us in finding the stronghold, exposing and confronting the lie, and guiding the individual toward believing and embracing the truth of God's Word.

Personal and Spiritual Inventory Form

Counselees complete a Personal and Spiritual Inventory Form which is entirely confidential (see appendix). It is designed around Neil Anderson's Confidential Personal Inventory.[9] The form gathers information from the following areas: personal data, relational history, physical health, and spiritual health.

This Personal and Spiritual Inventory Form may surprise us with relevant information. We save precious time by having the counselee answer these questions in writing rather than gathering this information verbally. I explain its purpose to counselees, provide instruction in how to properly complete the form, and take time to examine it with them when they are done. This provides me with an opportunity to assess their non-verbal reactions as well as clarify any unclear answers.

Learning as much as we can about the counselee prior to the actual deliverance process can help us determine the nature of the problem and which areas must be exposed to truth. Since the spiritual, mental, emotional, and physical aspects of life interact with one another, we want to deal with the whole person, not just one part of them. Knowing that Satan operates in various areas of one's life, gathering information in these areas is useful for determining the who, what, when, where, and why of a particular situation.

Personal Data

Personal data simply lists an individual's name, address, telephone number, church affiliation, educational level, occupation, and other basic information needed for record keeping, accuracy, and communication.

Relational History

The relational history category provides valuable background data and alerts us to possible ancestral entry points. It is wise to ascertain if the counselee's great-grandparents, grandparents, or parents have ever been involved in occultic, cultic, or non-Christian religious practices. Counselees simply circle or place a check mark by any item they determine to be a part of their relational history.

Be certain to answer any questions they may have regarding the meaning of terms. Sometimes counselees are familiar with the experience, but not the proper term attached to that experience.

Discover the religious impact of their parents. Were they believers? Did they actively and obediently follow Christ or was their walk incongruent with their talk? Did the parents exhibit a vibrant and dynamic relationship with the Lord or were they uninterested in spiritual and religious details? Listening to others discuss the religious impact of their parents has taught me just how great an influence parents can have in the lives of their children.

Are the parents divorced or are they still married? Were there problems of sexual immorality within the home such as adulterous affairs, incestuous relationships, or problems with pornography? Were they adopted? Discuss the roles of both the father and mother. Who was the head of the household? How did the parents treat one another?

Exploring the moral atmosphere of adolescent and teenage years provides information surrounding the moral climate in of childhood years. Were the parents overly strict, overly lax, or well balanced? The area of morality could include the following items: the clothing they were allowed to wear, sexual activity, dating rules and regulations, movies they were allowed to attend, television programs they were allowed to watch, attitudes toward drinking, smoking, and drugs, church attendance, music listened to, books read, and the freedom to choose their own way.

The questions and statements on this form are never used to satisfy personal curiosity about counselees in order to know every detail of their life. They are to be used for the sole purpose of gathering pertinent information toward the process of finding freedom from demonic bondage. An understanding of the counselee's relational history may prove beneficial in diagnosing an entry point or stronghold arising from a particular event or experience.

Physical History

The physical history of the counselee should also be considered. We are not medical doctors and do not pretend to be so. We do not diagnose medical conditions or prescribe medication or release one from medication. We are merely trying to discover possible entry points through which demons have entered.

The counselee's personal health history should encompass both the physical and mental domain. Are they eating a balanced diet or do they feast on junk food? Do they experience uncontrolled cravings? Are they presently seeing a medical doctor and what medications are they presently taking? Do they experience difficulty sleeping or encounter bad dreams? What do they do for relaxation?

Because one of the primary battle grounds in spiritual warfare involves the mind, discuss the mental health of the counselee and discover what thoughts they are presently struggling with such as lust, inferiority, worry, etc. A checklist of these items helps them easily identify such thoughts.

Investigate what comes through the eye gate and ear gate of their life. Do they watch a great deal of television? Which shows do they consider to be their favorite? What magazines and books do they like to read? What kind of music do they listen to?

Is their general outlook on life positive or negative? What emotions are they having difficulty controlling or expressing? How do they handle the emotions they feel? Do they have a friend they can share with in total honesty? Are they totally honest with their feelings before God? Are they ever plagued with evil thoughts? Do they feel as though there is a dialogue occurring in their mind with voices that are not their own?

Is there a history of addictive problems such as alcohol, drugs, sex, etc. Do physical problems reside in the family such as cancer, heart disease, diabetes, etc.? Is there a history of mental illness?

These questions may increase our ability to discern demonic entry points. For instance, it may be wise to explore the possibility of ancestral entry points for counselees who are adopted and do not know their biological family history. An addiction to alcohol could be an entry point and stronghold for Satan. A propensity to watch vile and immoral television shows is an area worth exploring, etc. These questions offer you a knowledge base from which to start the process.

It must again be pointed out that we are not in any way attempting to play the role of a medical doctor. We are only asking these questions in order to form a knowledge base from which to start the process. We are uncovering relevant clues toward solving the harassment puzzle.

Spiritual Health

The spiritual health of the counselee is, or course, one of the most important categories to investigate. If the counselee has not made a conscious decision to embrace the way of Christ, then sharing the good news of salvation is essential.

The following two questions function as a spiritual stethoscope in helping to diagnose the inner condition of the heart: 1) If you were to die right now would you go to be with God in heaven? 2) If you did die right now, and were standing before the entrance gate of heaven and God said to you, "Why should I let you into My heaven?" how would you answer Him?

The response to the first question alerts us to their assurance of salvation while the second question reveals their understanding of the means of salvation. Are they basing their salvation upon meritorious works or solely upon the work of Christ on Calvary?

Since we were born into this world inherently sinful, no amount of good deeds allow us to measure up to God's holy standard of perfection. This is where the work of Christ comes into the picture. Ephesians 2:8-9 clearly states, "For by grace you have been saved through faith; and that not of yourselves, it is a gift of God; not as a result of works, that no one should boast."

Even though our salvation comes by grace through faith, we should not let good deeds fall by the wayside. Ephesians 2:10 goes on to say, "For we are His workmanship, created in Christ Jesus for good works, which God prepared beforehand, that we should walk in them." Good works are the *by-products* of a dynamic, vibrant relationship with God and are not the *basis* for our salvation.

Have counselees describe the details (where, when, how, etc.) of their salvation experience. Are they presently involved in a local church fellowship? Do they support the church with their time, talents, and finances?

Explore their devotion to regular Bible reading and study. Are they in the habit of prayer? Do they sense demonic harassment when praying, reading the Bible, worshiping God, or attending church services?

Finally, explore any personal involvement with cultic, occultic, or non-Christian phenomenon. Have they ever been hypnotized, participated in a seance, been involved in the "New Age" movement, or explored the area of parapsychology?

3. SETTING THE TONE

After gathering pertinent information, another counseling appointment may be scheduled at a later time or the counseling session may begin immediately. Scheduling a later appointment 1) offers us time for further personal preparation, 2) allows us to carefully sift through the counselee's responses, and 3) the extra time may prove beneficial in helping the counselee uncover additional information not shared during the initial session.

However, waiting could produce insurmountable fear so they will never come back for the second appointment. Additionally, they may be so severely harassed by demons that immediate attention is needed. Personal judgment should be used for this decision and will largely depend upon the severity of their problem, and their response to the Personal and Spiritual Inventory Form.

It has been my practice to keep the process intact as much as possible. Taking break periods during the sessions is helpful, but stretching the process out too long can fracture any prior progress made. As much as possible, I like to finish what I began.

When we do meet to continue the process, whether it is immediate or scheduled for a later date, the third step in the deliverance process involves setting the tone for this meeting. In this step, we are managing the atmosphere, informing the individual of the process, and establishing parameters upon evil spirits. We are taking charge of the situation.

Personal Awareness

Inform counselees of what you will be doing, what might occur in the process, and secure their permission to proceed. It is both spiritually profitable and morally correct to ensure that counselees are aware of the process upon which they are entering. Since defeating Satan involves exercising our rightful authority, counselees must learn to do this on their own during the process.

It is not unusual for demonized individuals to entertain evil thoughts or hear the voices of demons speaking to them and to each other. If this occurs, ask the counselee to immediately bring these thoughts out in the open. Satan will besiege the mind with lies in order to bring about confusion and fear. Since God operates openly and on the basis of truth, there is absolutely nothing to hide.

Observing the power of Scripture in action is one of the most exciting aspects of the process. God's truth never fails! As counselees bring out into the open the deceptive thoughts Satan places in their minds, his lies are exposed by the powerful Word of God. Deception is the opposite of truth. Lies flourish where truth is absent. Once exposed by the truth, the grip of deception is broken.

Demons often place the following thoughts in the minds of counselees which must be brought into the open and dealt with:

I will kill you if you go through with this.

I will harm one of your beloved friends or relatives.

This is totally unnecessary and involves needles pain and embarrassment.

Do not trust counselors. They do not have your best interest in mind and only want to bring you harm.

You are a lot better off with the pain you are experiencing now, than with the pain I will bring to you if you continue.

When their inner thoughts are brought out in the open and compared with the truth of Scripture, counselees become active participants in the process and Satan's deception is rendered impotent.

In order to separate Satan's lies from one's own thoughts, it is necessary for counselees to verbally express the thoughts they are experiencing and/or the voices they are hearing.

In an attempt to catch us off guard and get us to back down, demons will react in ways they hope will surprise, confuse, and frighten us. The counselee may experience difficulty in breathing, fall into a catatonic state, exhibit immense anxiety and fear, or become violent. Do not allow the demons to do this. Remember, they are under your delegated authority and must obey.

During one particular counseling session, the counselee began to choke and gasp for air. Something had her by the neck and was choking her. Realizing it was an attempt to bring fear into the process, I commanded the demon to immediately stop and her breathing returned to normal.

After explaining the procedure to the individual, commit the entire meeting to the control of the Holy Spirit through prayer. Verbally acknowledge His presence and power and ask Him to lead and guide the process for the glory of God. Even though we possess delegated authority from above, we still need divine insight in using it to the best of our ability. Delegated authority, in conjunction with the divine guidance of the Holy Spirit, becomes an unparalleled dynamic duo.

Drawing Boundary Lines

Take time to bind the enemy. This can be done in several ways. Reiterate your victory over them based upon the death and resurrection of Jesus Christ. They were defeated at the Cross!

Tell the demons that they must obey your commands to them and that they are not allowed to interfere with the thought processes of the counselee. They are not to call for reinforcements or communicate with other spirits. I do not allow them to speak to me, unless I first speak to them.

This is a great time to pray the truth of Scripture through doctrinal prayers. In other words, we are clearly stating the authority upon which we are acting and what parameters we are placing upon the demons. As children of God, we have the right and the authority to be in charge. Let the demons know who they are up against and the parameters to which they must must adhere.

Some feel it is profitable to engage in conversations with demons, but I believe it is best to keep this to a minimum. There may be occasions when we have to speak directly with them, but the goal is for counselees to learn how to confront demons on their own. Counselees must be active participants in the process.

Since the nature of demons is to lie and deceive, if we do speak directly with them, always ask if their reply will stand as truth before the throne of God.

Binding demons means to utilize and exercise our delegated authority in Christ to control and limit their behavior. Counselees should not passively sit in a trance while demons use their body and voice to communicate. We can exert our authority and control demonic behavior while counselees are cognitively active in the process. Bind the demons and deal directly with the person.

Although demons know they must obey, they often do so kicking and screaming all the way. They test us to see if we are merely *talking* about our authority or if we really know how to utilize it. If they should raise their ugly heads in defiance, and they will, we simply use our authority delegated to us from Christ and command them to obey.

4. DEALING WITH TRUTH AND SIN ISSUES

Dealing with truth and sin issues is where the rubber meets the road and the real grappling takes place. This step confronts the lie, or sin, which gave Satan his foothold, and asks the counselee to renounce it and embrace the truth. This is the heart of discovering open doors for demonic activity and slamming them shut with the truth of Scripture.

As leaders of this process, it is imperative that we not do this for the counselee. Counselees should verbally renounce the stronghold, repent from sin, embrace the truth, and declare that Satan no longer has a right to their life. If the demon attempts to come back, as is often the case, the counselee will be able to take control of the situation. Counselees must learn to exercise their own delegated authority. It is like teaching a baby to walk. Once they get the hang of it, they are off and running.

Renounce Evil and Affirm Truth

I usually begin this step by asking counselees to verbally declare total rejection of Satan and his involvement in their life, and announce a desire to follow God's truth. When this is done, demons realize they are in serious trouble as their safe haven in a passive and deceived individual is over. The counselee has taken the bold step of telling them they are no longer wanted.

Next, I proceed with items from the Personal and Spiritual Inventory Form that raise a caution flag in my mind. Ask the counselee to renounce all involvement, past and present, with each problem area and then confess any sin to God, and seek His cleansing as promised in 1 John 1:9.

For instance, if an individual is involved in the occult, he/she will want to renounce that involvement as sinful, repent of all connection to it, seek forgiveness from God, and verbally declare to Satan that he no longer has a right to that portion of his/her life. Rather than a blanket renunciation which covers everything, I insist that counselees state precisely what they are renouncing and specifically declare to Satan that his claim to that particular stronghold has been removed.

Maybe the Personal and Spiritual Inventory Form reveals an addiction to a disgusting and filthy television show. That person should, 1) renounce it as being a tool of the enemy in their life, 2) verbally declare that they desire no part of it, 3) confess that it is not glorifying to God, 4) repent of the activity, 5) seek the forgiveness of Christ, and 6) affirm the truth of Scripture regarding holy living and the necessity of guarding the ear and eye gates.

Philippians 4:8 is an excellent passage to read and affirm:

> *Finally, brethren, whatever is true, whatever is honorable, whatever is right, whatever is pure, whatever is lovely, whatever is of good repute, if there is any excellence and if anything worthy of praise, let your mind dwell on these things.*

When counselees verbally do this for themselves, Satan knows they mean serious business! But if they are unwilling to participate in the process, they will never be able to withstand the enemy for themselves.

It is at this point where much of the resistance is encountered. Satan and his cohorts will do anything to keep this process from getting off the ground. The last thing they want to hear is the voice of their victim renouncing evil ways and reclaiming lost ground. They realize that the party is over.

While resistance may be strong in the beginning, demonic strength weakens considerably as each stronghold is renounced and there is no more ground upon which to stand.

At this particular point in the process, individuals sometimes experience extreme fear, difficulty in breathing, and memory blocks. Command the demons to immediately free the counselee from the difficulty and to obey your authoritative words. Remind them of their defeated position, your authority over them, and that they have no choice but to obey.

Demons are like rigid strands of spaghetti which become limp when soaked in water. They may stand firm at first, but they soon weaken when confronted with the powerful truth of God.

The process for helping someone find freedom from demonic bondage is not a quick three-step process. It takes time and energy to move through the various strongholds. It can become exhausting and breaks may be needed. Since it involves a human being in need of instruction, encouragement, counsel, and prayer, it should not be viewed with a microwave mentality. The process may demand a heavy allotment of time and can be emotionally draining. Yet, it is extremely rewarding to see the smile on an individual's face who has just experienced freedom from demonic harassment.

Key problem areas often involve pride, a lack of submission to God and to those in authority over us, and unforgiveness. In each of these areas, the process remains the same, expose the lie, renounce and repent, and affirm the truth.

Pride

A major obstacle to attaining a greater communion with God is pride. It is often the very thing that keeps us from doing what is right and walking more closely with our Lord. The ambitious pride of Satan was also involved in the original sin of the universe (Ezek. 16:49; 1 Tim. 3:6).

Pride deceives our hearts (Jer. 49:16), hardens our minds (Dan. 5:20), brings about trouble (Prov. 13:10), binds like a chain (Ps. 73:6), and accompanies destruction (Prov. 16:18).

Arrogance of the heart produces strife, while the heart depending on the Lord prospers (Prov. 28:25). It is foolish to trust in oneself, but we walk wisely when we trust in the Lord (Prov. 28:26).

God hates pride (Prov. 6:17; 1 Pet. 5:1-10). It is an abomination unto the Lord (Prov. 16:5) and He opposes it (Jam. 4:6). Those absorbed in pride will surely stumble and fall (Jer. 50:32).

Though Satan himself is filled with pride and tries to fill our hearts with arrogance, God desires that we exercise humility. Humility is not self-deprecation or the maintaining of a "worm" theology, it is actually placing our confidence solidly in God and not in ourselves.

God dwells with the humble (Is. 57:15) and requires that human beings walk humbly with Him (Mic. 6:8). Humility is at the heart of the incarnation. God humbled Himself when He took on the form of a human being (Phil. 2:7-8). Paul warns us not to think more highly of ourselves than we ought (Rom. 12:3) and also encourages a humility that counts others better than ourselves (Phil. 2:3). Jesus stated in Matthew 23:12, "And whoever exalts himself shall be humbled; and whoever humbles himself shall be exalted."

Another Scriptural passage which contrasts humility and pride is 1 Peter 5:5-6:

> *...and all of you, clothe yourselves with humility toward one another, for God is opposed to the proud, but gives grace to the humble. Humble yourselves, therefore, under the mighty hand of God, that He may exalt you at the proper time."*

Satan can easily deceive us into thinking that we are more important than we really are. By bringing pride into our lives, he skews our perception of reality. When the perception of ourselves and God is altered, our behavior and thoughts are out of line with God's Word. Warning us that pride is not from God, 1 John 2:16

states, "For all that is in the world, the lust of the flesh and the lust of the eyes and the boastful pride of life, is not from the Father, but is from the world."

We can do nothing of spiritual value unless we are humbly connected to Christ as John 15:4-5 states:

> *Abide in Me, and I in you. As the branch cannot bear fruit of itself, unless it abides in the vine, so neither can you, unless you abide in Me. I am the vine, you are the branches; he who abides in Me, and I in him, he bears much fruit; for apart from Me you can do nothing.*

If deception and bondage have occurred because of an abundance of pride and a lack of humility, then initiate the process of cleansing with counselees. Renounce specific areas of pride, agree with God regarding its wicked influence, seek His forgiveness, affirm the truth of Scripture, and clothe yourself with humility.

Rebellion Against Authority

Another realm of frequent deception and bondage surrounds the area of submission to those in authority. The prevalent "me-first" mindset so evident in our culture, combined with an "I'll do it my way," attitude, leads to a rebellious spirit.

It almost goes without saying that Satan has viciously bombarded the church on this point. Pastors scratch their heads wondering why no one listens to them while church members raise their eyebrows in amazement saying, "They just don't make pastors like they used to." Respect and submission are at an all-time low.

Even the motive for attending church services is eroding under the gale force winds of rebellion. Most Christians do not view themselves as being rebellious. To mention this possibility would come as a surprise and insult to them. Yet, the pattern is the same. We criticize the pastor, criticize the music, criticize the sermon, criticize the entire service because it was not organized the way we thought it should be. Instead of entering into worship, we critique the service. As subtle as it may be, many have succumbed to this deceptive act of rebellion.

Not only does Satan deceive us into subtle rebellion, sometimes we blatantly rebel against God and others in authority. Christians come in all different sizes and shapes and also possess varying levels of spiritual maturity, from babes in Christ to mature followers.

Rebellion exists when we begin to pick and choose which Scriptures to follow. Those parts about forgiveness, spiritual giftedness, and God's care over us are exciting and palatable, but serving others, sharing Christ with our neighbors, and contributing financially to the Kingdom of God often get filed in the "That's not for me," drawer.

During one of my pastorates, an elder in the church provided this rationale for not contributing to the ministry of the local congregation of which he was a leader. He said, "The Bible says that God loves a cheerful giver and since I do not give cheerfully, I have decided not to give at all. If I gave without being cheerful, I would be dishonoring God." He disguised his excuse in religious garb, but it was merely a rebellious rationalization which really meant, "I will pick and choose which Scriptures I want to follow."

God, the Creator and Sustainer of the universe has established lines of authority; children submit to parents, employees submit to employers, believers submit to spiritual leaders, civilians submit to governments, etc. God, Who possesses all knowledge and occupies the seat of eternal wisdom, surely must have known what He was doing when He told us to submit to His divine order. In essence, rebelling against those in authority is actually rebelling against God. Submitting to those in authority is an act of submitting to God and obeying His Word.

Satan is no stranger to rebellion. His arrogant pride led him to rebel against God in heaven. The reason we experience spiritual warfare now is because Satan is still exercising rebelliousness toward God. Satan's private war has invaded this realm and the consequences have been enormous.

Before we experienced the forgiveness of Christ, we were rebellious enemies in the kingdom of darkness, altogether alienated from the true and holy God. Without the work of Christ at Calvary, we would still be His enemies. Everything there is about rebellion, whether its expressions are veiled or blatant, is totally opposite of God's ways. It is so disgusting that our Lord likens it to the sin of witchcraft in 1 Samuel 15:23, "For rebellion is as the sin of divination, and insubordination is as iniquity and idolatry."

The following passages speak of a divinely established order of godly submission:

Civil Authorities:

Romans 13:1-5
Let every person be in subjection to the governing authorities. For there is no authority except from God, and those which exist are established by God. Therefore he who resists authority has opposed the ordinance of God; and they who have opposed will receive condemnation upon themselves. For rulers are not a cause of fear for good behavior, but of evil. Do you want to have no fear of authority? Do what is good, and you will have praise from the same; for it is a minister of God to you for good. But if you do what is evil, be afraid; for it does not bear the sword for nothing; for it is a minister of God, an avenger who brings wrath upon the one who practices evil. Wherefore it is necessary to be in subjection, not only because of wrath, but also for conscience' sake.

1 Peter 2:13-17
Submit yourselves for the Lord's sake to every human institution, whether to a king as one in authority, or to governors as sent by him for the punishment of evildoers and the praise of those who do right. For such is the will of God that by doing right you may silence the ignorance of foolish men. Act as free men, and do not use your freedom as a covering for evil, but use it as bondslaves of God. Honor all men; love the brotherhood, fear God, honor the king.

Are there incidents or areas where the counselee is rebelling against civil authorities? The Bible requires that we pray for our human leaders and submit to them. The only time for civil disobedience is when we are required to engage in, or support, something that is morally wrong before God.

Information gained from the Personal and Spiritual Inventory Form will prove helpful in identifying areas of rebellion, but paying close attention to the attitude of the counselee, what they say and how they say it, also provides valuable clues to the condition of the inner heart. Being sensitive to the Holy Spirit's leading is also crucial in determining possible areas of rebellion.

Children and Parents:

Ephesians 6:1-3
Children, obey your parents in the Lord, for this is right. Honor your father and mother (which is the first commandment with a promise), that it may be well with you, and that you may live long on the earth.

We tend to accept teenage rebellion as one of those difficult times in life we all must endure. I suspect that the problem is not only a child's blatant disrespect for this commandment, but also in the way we parent. Realizing the role of parents in this interaction, Ephesians 6:4 goes on to say, "And, fathers, do not provoke your children to anger; but bring them up in the discipline and instruction of the Lord."

Every year after returning from a week long church camp during the summer months, my parents vowed never to send us there again. We came home on a spiritual high that made us virtually impossible to live with. We forgot that obeying our parents was one of the ingredients toward pleasing God.

Do counselees exhibit a rebellious spirit toward their parents? Are the parents rebelling against God's command to bring their children up in the Lord without provoking them to anger? Could these be active ingredients in the rebellion so often seen in the young people of today?

I have seen parents go overboard with the obedience issue. They pontificate from their parental throne and demand that their children obey every decree from their lips. The obedience they receive is not based on love and respect for the parent, it is based on fear. Fear will dominate where love is lacking. Rebellion and submission with regard to both the parent and the child is an area well worth exploring for possible demonic strongholds.

Husbands and Wives:

1 Peter 3:1-7
In the same way, you wives, be submissive to your own husbands so that even if any of them are disobedient to the word, they may be won without a word by the behavior of their wives, as they observe your chaste and respectful behavior. And let not your adornment be merely external–braiding the hair, and wearing gold jewelry, or putting on dresses; but let it be the hidden person of the heart, with the imperishable quality of a gentle and quiet spirit, which is precious in the sight of God. For in this way in former times the holy women also, who hoped in God, used to adorn themselves, being submissive to their own husbands. Thus Sarah obeyed Abraham, calling him lord, and you have become her children if you do what is right without being frightened by any fear. You husbands likewise, live with your wives in an understanding way, as with a weaker vessel, since she is a woman; and grant her honor as a fellow heir of the grace of life, so that your prayers may not be hindered.

Ephesians 5:22-31
Wives, be subject to your own husbands, as to the Lord. For the husband is the head of the wife, as Christ also is the head of the church, He Himself being the Savior of the body. But as the church is subject to Christ, so also the wives ought to be to their husbands in everything. Husbands, love your wives, just as Christ also loved the church and gave Himself up for her; that He might sanctify her, having cleansed her by the washing of water with the word, that He might present to Himself the church in all her glory, having

no spot or wrinkle or any such thing; but that she should be holy and blameless. So husbands ought also to love their own wives as their own bodies. He who loves his own wife loves himself; for no one ever hated his own flesh, but nourishes and cherishes it, just as Christ also does the church, because we are members of His body. For this cause a man shall leave his father and mother, and shall cleave to his wife; and the two shall become one flesh.

Whenever we take two people with different backgrounds, different educational levels, different personalities, different perspectives, and different, different, different, there are bound to be areas of difficulty. Difficulties experienced at home usually spill over into every other area of our life. It is easy for Satan to sneak into marital hardships and establish a foothold.

Employer and Employee:

1 Peter 2:18-21
Servants, be submissive to your masters with all respect, not only to those who are good and gentle, but also to those who are unreasonable. For this finds favor, if for the sake of conscience toward God a man bears under sorrows when suffering unjustly. For what credit is there if, when you sin and are harshly treated, you endure it with patience? But if when you do what is right and suffer for it you patiently endure it, this finds favor with God.

Ephesians 6:5
Slaves, be obedient to those who are your masters according to the flesh, with fear and trembling, in the sincerity of your heart, as to Christ.

Not every employer is a joy to work for because some are evil and nasty. There is nothing wrong with moving upward and onward in our employment status, but the bottom line in any job is an honest day's work with an attitude that is pleasing to the Lord. This area could easily be overlooked for demonic strongholds.

Spiritual Leaders:

Hebrews 13:17
Obey your leaders, and submit to them; for they keep watch over your souls, as those who will given an account. Let them do this with joy and not with grief, for this would be unprofitable for you.

This is perhaps one of the harder Scriptural passages for believers to incorporate. Christians tend to equate their high involvement in the church with the right to dictate how things are done. Often the concept of stewardship is replaced with the concept of ownership. When an ownership mentality takes over, it is easy to rationalize disobedience to God's command.

Below are typical rationalizations for a lack of submission:

I'll submit when he starts to change his ways.

He's unfit to even be in the ministry.

How are we expected to submit when he is not a godly person?

He doesn't have the right to do what he is doing so we can't submit.

I don't like him so I won't follow him.

Have you ever used any of these lines? The list of rationalizations go on and on, but each displays an inner rebellion against a submissive, humble, and servant spirit which Christ so vividly exemplified. It is true that leaders can, and do at times, abuse their spiritual authority, but in the majority of instances, people just find it difficult to submit.

Without doubt, Satan has established a fortress of rebellion in the hearts of many believers. If things do not go our way and are not carried out in the manner that we think best, then submission is not forthcoming. Instead of simple obedience to God's Word, our submission becomes conditional upon who we like, how things go, and how much input we are allowed. To neglect exploring this realm of potential strongholds can be hazardous to the health of the church, and the individual.

Bitterness and Unforgiveness

One of the most frequently traveled avenues for demonic strongholds is the road of bitterness and unforgiveness. Paul admonishes us in 2 Corinthians 2:10-11, to forgive others so that Satan cannot take advantage of us:

> *But whom you forgive anything, I forgive also; for indeed what I have forgiven, if I have forgiven anything, I did it for your sakes in the presence of Christ, in order that no advantage be taken of us by Satan; for we are not ignorant of his schemes.*

A poignant lesson on forgiveness is presented in Matthew 18 where a servant who did not practice forgiveness was turned over to the tormentors. The impact of this story is felt in verse 35 when Jesus declares, "So shall My heavenly Father also do to you, if each of you does not forgive his brother from your heart."

The point often overlooked is that God will treat us in a similar manner if we do not extend to others the forgiveness which we ourselves have experienced. The forgiveness we are to extend is unlimited (Mt.18:21-22). Forgiveness experienced and forgiveness extended must be congruent with one another. Ephesians 4:31-32 clearly states our obligation:

> *Let all bitterness and wrath and anger and clamor and slander be put away from you, along with all malice. And be kind to one another, tender-hearted, forgiving each other, just as God in Christ also has forgiven you.*

God did not confer upon us what we justly deserved, instead He looked upon us with mercy and extended His forgiveness to us. In light of this fact, being merciful as God has shown mercy is expected of His followers (Lk. 6:36).

Forgiveness is often equated with forgetting as suggested in the well known phrase "forgive and forget." But forgiving and forgetting are entirely different. Requiring the two to go together frustrates people because, try as we might, we cannot always forget.

While we are vehemently reminded in Scripture to forgive one another, I know of nowhere in the Bible where we are told to forget in the sense of experiencing memory loss.

Paul says that he is "forgetting what lies behind and reaching forward to what lies ahead" (Phil. 3:13), but this does not mean he cannot remember the past. The context reveals that he is not allowing his past to hinder him from being and doing all that God desires. Even when Isaiah said in 43:18, "Do not call to mind the former things, or ponder things of the past," it is obvious that ceasing to remember is not what he had in mind. If we wipe the past from our memory, why would Isaiah counsel against pondering what we supposedly are unable to remember?

Hebrews 10:17 informs us that God remembers our sin no more. Many feel that if God forgets, we should too. But if God is omniscient (knows all things) and omnipresent (is everywhere present) how is it that He can forget? To forget would imply that He no longer is all knowing and would thus cease to be God. This is absurd! There must be an explanation.

When God forgives us, He does not forget in the sense that His memory is blank. Have you ever walked into the kitchen, stopped, and could not remember why you went in there? God does not forget in that sense. If He did, we would be in great trouble. What if He forgot to write our name in the Book of Life? What if He did not remember that we are His children? What if He did not remember His promises to us in Scripture?

When the Bible states that God remembers our sin no more, it means that He does not count our sin against us. When we bring up past instances that we have supposedly forgiven, and hold them against others, it is a sign that we have not truly forgiven them.

The most common word for forgiveness in the New Testament is "aphesis." As a noun it occurs 15 times while the verb occurs approximately 40 times. The Greek word "aphesis" conveys the meaning of "letting go" or "releasing" something. Forgiveness is not holding another person's sin against them, thus we release them and let them go.

Practically speaking, forgiveness is a willingness to live with the consequences of another person's sin. It is costly, but this is exactly how Jesus forgave us. He took the consequences of our sin upon Himself and ended up dying for that act. This arduous task weighed so heavily upon His shoulders that in the Garden of Gethsemane He sweat drops of blood while confirming His Father's will (Mt. 26; Mk. 14; Lk. 22). In essence, forgiveness is substitutional in nature because no one really forgives without bearing the penalty of the other person's sin.

God never requires us to do something which is impossible for us to accomplish. If we *could not* forgive, He would be setting us up for failure. But He does not teach us to swim, only to let us drown. Truly forgiving someone from the heart is not only something that *ought* to be done, it is also something that *can* be done. When forgiveness is extended, our soul is freed for a closer walk with the God who has forgiven us.

Forgiving someone is not an easy task. Our concept of justice and the need to forgive are always wrestling with each other. Since others have deeply hurt us, we may want them to suffer for the pain they have created. Revenge is not the Christian way as Romans 12:19 notes, "Never take your own revenge, beloved, but leave room for the wrath of God, for it is written, 'vengeance is mine, I will repay,' says the Lord."

When others wrong us and hurt us, we let them off *our* hook, but they never get off *God's* hook. Even though we release them, they will answer to Him someday. Since we are not all knowing as God is, even if we were allowed revenge, it would not be truly just. Only God is able to execute true justice.

When others hurt us, Satan wants that pain to grow into bitterness so he can gain a stronghold in our life. When our pain is not taken to the Lord in prayer, it can fester like a sore that never heals.

When bitterness is present, forgiveness is absent.

Unforgiveness costs us dearly in many ways. It adversely affects our physical bodies. We can actually experience physical pain and problems because of an unwillingness to extend forgiveness. It also adversely affects our emotional well being. Anger and bitterness cooped up inside can create inner turmoil that will wreak havoc in our thought life. Finally, unforgiveness adversely affects our spiritual life. How can we experience the jubilant communion of a forgiving God when we ourselves are unable to forgive?

We do not forgive others merely for their sake, for they may or may not accept our forgiveness. Forgiveness is also extended for our sake, so we can be free or demonic strongholds and free to experience the richness of God in our lives. Forgiveness is ultimately an issue between ourselves and God.

When leading someone to freedom from bitterness, the reality of pain and suffering experienced by the counselee is not to be dismissed. The hurt they encountered is very real. Feelings and emotions must be validated. When forgiveness does not reach the heart of one's emotions, it is usually incomplete.

On a sheet of paper, I ask counselees to write down 1) the name of every person to whom they should extend forgiveness, and 2) the name of every person they have offended and should seek forgiveness. Together we pray for God's Spirit to bring to mind every name that should be on the list. Then, beside each name, we write the specific reason, action, or occurrence of why forgiveness is needed.

We then work our way down the list of specific names and specific actions praying, "Lord, I forgive (so and so) for (list the specific offense)." This can be a very emotional and painful time because of such deep wounds. Many of the offenses endured are horrifying. Since pain involves our emotions, and forgiveness involves releasing others from the pain they have inflicted, the Kleenex box should be readily accessible.

I have watched grown adults weep while releasing the bitterness, anger, and unforgiveness cooped up inside them for years. When they have finished and the tissues have run out, they smile with radiant joy. For the first time in their life, they know what it means to be free. The absence of bitterness makes room for more of God's love.

When evil strongholds have been demolished and ground once occupied by demons has been authoritatively taken back, ask counselees how they feel. Despite the fact that they are weak from such an emotionally draining experience, there will be an aura of excitement about them as they sense the peace and freedom of Christ. They are now free to vigorously pursue spiritual growth.

Freedom from demonic bondage may include the following:

1. Freedom from physical problems. If an illness is caused by demons, then that illness will leave when the demons go.

2. Counselees exhibit a new understanding and awareness of demonic strongholds and the power of God.

3. A loss of supernatural power. If powers were obtained through the occult, a renunciation of those practices can mean a loss of demon induced power.

4. A return of an illness. If healing came about by demonic power, then the illness may return when the evil power no longer has control.

Before leaving the session, allow time for thanksgiving and praise to God for His deliverance. Sing songs unto the Lord, read Scriptural passages of praise, and provide the counselee an opportunity to personally thank God. All glory, honor, and praise is directed to Him for His victory. By glorifying God, we accomplish the very thing Satan despises.

5. POST-DELIVERANCE CARE

To help counselees maintain their freedom from demonic strongholds, post-deliverance care is absolutely essential. This step allows us to 1) explain further the importance of persevering and maintaining victory, and 2) provide a system of support for transitioning into victorious Christian living.

Freedom and Maturity

Making a clear distinction between the concept of freedom and the concept of maturity is essential. Confusing the two could lead to disaster. Freedom can be secured instantly because we are merely booting Satan from territory that is not rightfully his. Maturity, however, is a process which takes a great deal of time and effort. One can be instantly freed from demonic bondage, but spiritual maturity comes with time.

Now that counselees are free from demonic strongholds, they have a greater capacity for growth. The more they mature in Christ, the more proficient they will be with handling the enemy. They can take advantage of God's wondrous working in their life by renewing their commitment to serve Him and know Him more fully.

There is no quick substitute for spiritual maturity. It involves hard work, self-discipline, and a willingness to dig deeper into God's Word.

Inform counselees that Satan will probably come around again seeking to take back his old ground (Mt. 12:43-45). If they do not know how to repel returning demons and preserve their freedom, then things may become worse than before. Rather than slip into old sinful ways, we want counselees to be prepared and ready to resist attacks. This is why they should be active participants in the entire process, rather than passive automatons. With God's strength and help, learning to stand on their own two feet against the enemy is absolutely essential for personal victory.

Live According to God's Truth

The importance of living one's life according to God's truth should also be discussed. By following God in obedience, no ground is yielded to Satan. When Satan has no ground for a stronghold, he has absolutely no claim to any part of our life.

Walking in obedience includes studying the Bible, communing with God by reading His Word and praying, continuing to confess instances of sin, seeking the forgiveness and cleansing of Christ, yielding the members of our body to the control and influence of the Holy Spirit, etc.

Help counselees realize and appropriate the power of their position in Christ. When an individual firmly grasps their new identity as a child of God, they are more apt to actually live out who they are declared to be.

Encourage counselees to practice daily the habit of praising God. Praise affirms His faithfulness and glorifies His name. Explain the need to daily take up and put on the armor of God. Help them identify and recognize old patterns of thinking and behavior by asking the Holy Spirit to control their lives. Instruct them to deal with Satanic attacks quickly, verbally, and authoritatively.

Obviously, this is far too much to cover at the end of an exhausting counseling session. Use judgment and discernment in determining just how much instruction is needed immediately after the session, but develop a follow-up system of support and discipling for counselees.

Since post-deliverance care will naturally extend beyond the actual deliverance session, link the individual up with someone of the same sex, who is knowledgeable in spiritual warfare, and who can act as an available and trustworthy mentor. This person can be a ready resource, a confidential prayer partner, and a disciple-maker who helps the counselee learn important principles of maintaining their freedom in Christ.

Post-deliverance Care Outline

1. *Praise God for the deliverance.*
   A. Discuss the glory issue.
   B. Ascribe glory to God through prayers of praise and thanksgiving.

2. *Distinguish maturity from freedom.*
   A. Freedom from demonic bondage can come instantly during the deliverance session.
   B. Spiritual maturity is a process that takes time and energy.
   C. Maturity means continued growth (2 Pet. 1:5-11).
      1) Commit oneself afresh to serving the Lord and knowing

Him better.

2) Satan will try to recover lost ground and they have to repel him.

3. *Steps for preserving one's freedom in Christ.*

A. Discuss the importance of living one's life in obedience to God's word.

B. Explain the daily need to:

1) Study and memorize Scripture.

2) Commune with God through prayer.

3) Take up and put on the armor of God.

4) Ascribe glory to God through praise and thanksgiving.

5) Yield oneself to the control and influence of the Holy Spirit so old habits and sinful patterns of thinking do not reign.

C. Create new understanding of their redeemed, powerful identity in Christ.

D. Recognize areas that are vulnerable to demonic attack.

E. Satan will return and try to reclaim lost ground.

1) Expose the lie with the truth of God's Word.

2) Exercise delegated authority by dealing with attacks quickly, verbally, and authoritatively.

3) When sin is present, confess it and seek forgiveness immediately.

F. Establish a proper support system needed for further growth.

1) Connect them with an available and trustworthy mentor.

N I N E

BEGINNING A FREEDOM MINISTRY

Because of the nature of the topic, it is unfortunate that many churches, through their teaching and behavior, place a huge sign on their ministry which says, "We don't do demons here." But the church should be involved in setting individuals free because freedom is the heart of what the gospel is all about.

While talk of Satan, demons, and deliverance may cause some to dismiss the need for helping believers find freedom from demonic oppression, it will inspire others toward greater awareness of the spiritual battle. If demonic influence through deception is a real possibility for believers, then establishing this kind of ministry within the local church could produce great results for the glory of God.

Because of the nature of the topic, it is unfortunate that many churches, through their teaching and behavior, place a huge sign on their ministry which says, "We don't do demons here." But the church should be involved in setting individuals free because freedom is what the gospel is all about.

There are individuals who are more interested in some sort of noxious high received from casting out demons than in actually helping people find freedom from demonic bondage. But I am not referring to weird, secret, late night meetings crawling with fear and ignorance. There is a need for a trained, and rational network of individuals within the church who are prepared to appropriately help the demonically oppressed. This type of ministry must involve a healthy, cerebral approach to ministry, not hype and hoopla.

Implementing an Outreach of Freedom

As with the introduction of most ministries, the support of church leadership is appropriate. To move ahead without the clear agreement and consensus of leadership is to ensure failure, or a weak ministry, which easily causes division and discord within the local church. With leadership on board, the ship will have an easier time leaving port and sailing toward its destination.

Once leadership is on board, preparing the congregation is a logical next step. Disseminating plenty of valuable, relevant, and accurate information is necessary for people to feel comfortable with the concept and understand what is happening and why the ministry is needed.

A small group may desire to study the issue and report back to the leadership board and the congregation within several months. This group of key individuals can study the issues, develop an understanding for dialogue, present a biblical basis for such a ministry, and introduce functional guidelines for its practice and implementation. When the ministry comes to fruition, the congregation will have full assurance that it has been entered into only after careful study and preparation.

To further raise awareness levels, pastors may conduct a preaching series on the topic, or bring in a guest speaker known for his/her knowledge in this area. An adult Sunday School class may be offered covering the armor of God, the believer's authority, Satan's deceptive schemes, etc.

Sunday evenings are excellent opportunities for discussing the ministry specifics and promoting questions and feedback. The church bulletin, newsletter, or other printed material may also be utilized as a means of reducing fears.

As with all activities, someone must oversee and organize this ministry or the likelihood of its success will diminish. It may be possible to establish ministry teams of three to five individuals. Some within the group are fully trained, while one or two are in the training process.

Since this type of ministry is looking for mature people, gifted and called for this specific ministry, selection criteria should be developed to ensure quality and credibility. This outreach could even be divided into two distinct ministry teams, one tackles the actual deliverance, while the other team focuses primarily on post-deliverance care and discipleship.

After the ministry is organized to best fit the needs of your church, the next step is training. Consistently read the Bible, pray, and keep up with new books on the subject. While this will expand your mind, it is no substitute for actual ministry involvement. Training should include both cognitive and practical knowledge.

Once the leadership is giving solid support, appropriate information has been disseminated, the outreach has been adequately organized and structured, and qualified volunteers are trained for service, free those volunteers for ministry. It is frustrating to have an area of responsibility without the freedom to pursue success.

Obviously, these are broad brush strokes on the canvas of ministry development. All of this takes time and much more detail should be developed by your particular church, but it is a starting point for implementing an outreach of freedom.

Recommendations for a Freedom Ministry

Because fear, confusion, and misunderstanding usually accompany the topic of spiritual warfare, the following recommendations and statements should be considered before beginning a deliverance ministry.

1. *Solidify commitment from key players prior to establishing a local church ministry.*

   Any ministry begun without support from influential leaders in the congregation will likely fall flat on its face. Work with key players so they understand the nature of spiritual warfare and the potential impact of this ministry.

2. *Information dilutes ignorance and fear.*

   Typically, the more people know about a subject, the less they fear it. Do all you can to promote understanding and awareness. Give people an opportunity to respond to the idea. Without the proper dissemination of adequate information, our own people will become our worst obstacle.

3. Keep our knowledge of the field current.

Make every effort to continue growing and learning about the subject. Read books and articles, attend workshops and seminars, and bring the best available resources to those involved. This keeps them on the cutting edge of ministry knowledge and effectiveness.

4. A deliverance ministry is not, and should not be, the primary focus of the church.

When one specific ministry takes over the focus of the church, it becomes unbalanced. Balance is the key word. Continue proclaiming the gospel, teaching from Scripture, offering music programs, evangelistic outreach, etc. Healthy churches maintain a balancc to their ministries.

5. Extreme emotionalism and subjectivism should be avoided in a deliverance ministry.

Deliverance can be calm, rational, and controlled. It involves the systematic removing of strongholds. Prancing about trying to "out-shout" the devil is ridiculous.

6. Pride and control issues among ministry volunteers are a hindrance to the ministry.

It is easy to puff ourselves up and imagine that we have some innate ability to control demons. This type of thinking is deceptive. Pride and control disrupts the ministry, takes glory away from God, and is used of Satan to turn a work designed against him, to actually work for him. The central purpose of the ministry is to set individuals free, not to flaunt one's spirituality or dogma. Only Jesus Christ can set people free. We are merely vessels in His hands.

7. Not everything is caused by a demon.

Build a network of professionals to whom you can refer individuals requiring help beyond what you can provide. We may not be able to help every person because 1) not everything is caused by a demon, and 2) we are not trained in everything. When someone needs additional help, feel free to refer them to trusted others with more knowledge, experience, and training.

8. *Deliverance ministry must be saturated with prayer.*

Prayer is a front line warfare activity that undergirds the effectiveness of the entire ministry. Without prayer support, fruitful ministry is limited.

9. *Evaluate the ministry on a regular basis.*

This should be done with all ministries. Regular evaluation allows us to monitor the ministry in terms of analyzing problems and assessing spiritual effectiveness. Evaluations help us to continually upgrade and improve the ministry.

10. *All glory goes to God.*

We are the branches and He is the vine. We are able to help the demonically oppressed because God is on our side. He deserves all of the glory and honor. A testimony from someone who has experienced freedom from demonic bondage can encourage the church and bring glory to God. It shows others, in a tangible way, how God can impact a life through this type of ministry.

Additional Items

Church unity is a unique factor of spiritual warfare which often escapes our notice. It acts as a protective devise against Satan, while disunity inflicts damage upon the church.

Kindling wood placed on a fire is quickly consumed. The little pieces, all separate from one another, allow the consuming flame to quickly spread. However, a large log placed on the fire takes the flame a great deal of time to burn.

This illustration suggests that when the followers of Christ are splintered and fractured, Satan has a much easier time consuming people, as kindling wood in the fire. But when a church is unified and in one accord, it acts like a huge log in the fireplace. Consider the local church you attend. Does unity and oneness abound or is it splintered and fractured as small kindling wood for Satan?

At times, houses, buildings, and specific places may need cleansing. One counselee was a bit anxious about returning to her home because she knew demons were occupying the house. A trusted friend from church accompanied her and together they went from room to room cleansing the house of demonic activity, claiming it for God, and dedicating it for His glory.

The Wilderness or Canaan

Most believers that I know really do want to live for God. They desire to make an impact in this world for Christ. So it is only appropriate that I close with an Old Testament illustration that challenges us toward becoming more involved in setting captives free and advancing the Kingdom of God against the enemy.

God promised the children of Israel that He would give them the land of Canaan and that His angel would go before them to drive the enemy away. God's ability to keep His promises was revealed through displays of power in Egypt, delivering the Hebrew children out of bondage to slavery, and providing victory over enemies and obstacles while on the way to Mount Sinai.

For the most part, Israel focused their attention on the negatives instead of the positives; the strength of their enemies instead of the power of God; the hardships along the wilderness journey instead of the wondrous promise of God toward new horizons. The result of such tunnel vision was 38 years of wandering around in the desert when they could have been in the promised land of Canaan.

Israel could have entered the promised land at Kadesh-Barnea. From there they could have easily conquered Canaan and claimed the inheritance God had secured for them. Instead of possessing what they could have had, and what God wanted for them, they aimlessly wandered in the wilderness.

Many Christians continually repeat Israel's mistake. Instead of obtaining victory from the hand of God, they wander about this life in a spiritual desert.

Some Christians do not mind wandering in the desert. After all, God provided Israel with manna to eat, clothes and shoes that did not wear out, and a pillar of cloud and fire to lead them.

Canaan was a different story. It involved fighting battles with the enemy, possessing and farming the land, and living in a strange and new territory. It involved risk, hard work, and a deeper faith in God. In some ways, it is easier to remain in the spiritual wilderness instead of heading toward Canaan.

Could it be that we are content to remain in the wilderness instead of experiencing the land of Canaan? Life is easy, consistent, and somewhat spiritually dull. We gather a little manna every Sunday morning during the worship service and put our time in with church activities. But too much talk about conquering Canaan means more work, and we are much too comfortable for that.

Keep in mind that Israel never won a battle because they possessed excellently trained soldiers with more weaponry and keen strategic planning. In most cases, the exact opposite was true. They won battles because God was on their side and He drove out the enemy. He was the factor that made the difference. He was their spiritual power.

It is also interesting to note that Israel was required to be a part of the battle. They did not sit back by the campfire warming themselves and singing merry melodies. They participated in the battle, even though their success depended upon the Lord.

It was probably very scary at times, knowing that from a human perspective, they did not really have a fighting chance for success. It was all God. They were simply obeying the Lord. All of the battles were different, from marching around a walled city blowing trumpets to holding up the arms of Moses. This was a constant reminder to them that victory always came by the hand of God.

The promised land scenario should encourage us to move toward Canaan instead of remaining in the wilderness. When we do pack our bags for the journey, we leave with the assurance that in spiritual warfare, it is always the Lord who makes the difference, for if God is for us, who can be against us?

Will you remain in your spiritual easy chair or will you begin to move out as God has planned? Life is much more rewarding and exciting in the land of Canaan!

Romans 8:31-39

> *What then shall we say to these things? If God is for us, who is against us? He who did not spare His own Son, but delivered Him up for us all, how will He not also with Him freely give us all things? Who will bring a charge against God's elect? God is the one who justifies; who is the one who condemns? Christ Jesus is He who died, yes, rather who was raised, who is at the right hand of God, who also intercedes for us. Who shall separate us from the love of Christ? Shall tribulation, or distress, or persecution, or famine, or nakedness, or peril, or sword? Just as it is written, "For Thy sake we are being put to death all day long; we were considered as sheep to be slaughtered." But in all these things we overwhelmingly conquer through Him who loved us. For I am convinced that neither death, nor life, nor angels, nor principalities, nor things present, nor things to come, nor powers, nor height, nor depth, nor any other created thing, shall be able to separate us from the love of God, which is in Christ Jesus.*

APPENDIX

Personal and Spiritual Inventory Form

Strictly Confidential

1. Personal Data

Name: ______________________________

Telephone: H) ______________ O) ______________

Church Attendance/Membership:

Present: ______________________________

Past: ______________________________

Education and Training:

Highest Grade Completed: ______________________________

Degrees Earned: ______________________________

Special Training: ______________________________

Marital Status:

Single ________ Married ________ Divorced ________

Marital History: ______________________________

____

Employment History:

Present: ______________________________

Past: ______________________________

Other Personal Data: ______________________________

____

2. *Relational History*

Were your parents believers? ______________________________

Describe the religious experience of your parents.

Are your parents currently married or divorced? ______________

Were there problems of sexual immorality within the home such as adulterous affairs, incestuous relationships, pornography? Explain.

Who was the head of the household? Explain.

How did your parents treat one another? Explain.

Discuss the roles of both your father and mother.

Are you adopted? ____

In thinking about the moral atmosphere in your home while growing up, rate each of the following areas accordingly:

5 = Very Permissive
4 = Permissive
3 = Average
2 = Strict
1 = Overly Strict

________	A.	Clothing
________	B.	Sexual Activity
________	C.	Dating
________	D.	Movies
________	E.	Television Programs
________	F.	Drinking
________	G.	Smoking
________	H.	Drugs
________	I.	Church Attendance
________	J.	Music
________	K.	Reading (books, magazines, etc.)
________	L.	Freedom of Choice

3. *Physical Health*

Describe your eating habits? Do you maintain a balanced diet? Explain.

Do you experience uncontrolled cravings for such things as food, alcohol, sweets, etc.?

Are you presently seeing a medical doctor? Explain.

Are you presently on medication? Explain.

Do you experience bad dreams or problems with sleeping? Explain.

What do you do for relaxation?

What thoughts, if any, are you presently struggling with in your life?

______ A. Lust
______ B. Inferiority
______ C. Worry
______ D. Doubt
______ E. Obsessive thoughts
______ F. Fantasy thoughts
______ G. Insecurity/inadequacy
______ H. Others (please list below)

How much television do you watch during the week (in number of hours) and what shows are your favorite?

What magazines and books do you like to read?

What kind of music do you like to listen to?

In your opinion, do you tend to have a positive outlook on life or a negative one? Explain.

Describe how you handle the emotions you experience?

Do you have a friend you can share with? ____________________

Are you totally honest with your feelings before God? __________

Are you ever plagued with evil thoughts? Explain.

Do you ever hear voices in your mind as though a dialogue were occurring with voices that are not your own? Explain.

Is there a history of addiction in your family to alcohol, drugs, sex, etc.? Explain.

Is there a history of physical problems in your family such as cancer, heart disease, diabetes, etc.? Explain.

Is there a history of mental illness? Explain.

4. Spiritual Health

If you were to die right now would you go to be with God in heaven? ________ Yes ________ No

If you did die right now, and were standing before the entrance gate of heaven and God said to you, "Why should I let you into My heaven?" how would you answer Him?

If you can, please briefly describe the details of your conversion.

Do you regularly attend a local church? ___ Yes ___ No

Describe your involvement and support of the local church.

Do you regularly read the Bible? ________ Yes ________ No

Do you pray regularly? ________ Yes ________ No

Describe your habits with prayer and Bible study.

Do you ever sense demonic harassment when praying, reading the Bible, worshiping God, or attending church services? Explain.

Describe your personal involvement, if any, with cultic, occultic, or non-Christian phenomenon.

Have you ever been hypnotized, participated in a seance, been involved in the New Age, or explored parapsychology? Explain

Please circle the experiences in which you or a family member have personally been involved.

OCCULT EXPERIENCES

Astral projection
Ouija board
Table lifting
Speaking in a trance
Automatic writing
Visionary dreams
Telepathy
Ghosts
Materialization
Clairvoyance
Clairsentience
Fortune telling
Tarot cards
Palm reading
Astrology
Rod and Pendulum (dowsing)
Healing magnetism
Magic charming
Mental suggestions
Black and white magic
Blood pacts
Fetishism
Incubi and succubae (sexual spirits)
Others ______________________________

CULT RELIGIONS

Christian Science
Unity
Scientology

"The Local Church"
The Way International
Unification Church
Church of the Living Word
Mormonism
Jehovah Witness
Children of God
Swedenborgianism
Herbert W. Armstrong (Radio Church of God)
Unitarianism
Masons
New Age
Others ______________________________

OTHER RELIGIONS

Zen Buddhism
Hare Krishna
Bahaism
Rosicrucian
Science of the Mind
Science of Creative Intelligence
Hinduism
Transcendental Meditation
Yoga
Echkankar
Roy Masters
Silva Mind Control
EST
Father Divine
Theosophical Society
Islam
Black Muslim
Other ______________________________

NOTES

INTRODUCTION

1. C.S. Lewis, *The Screwtape Letters*, Rev. Ed., (New York, NY: Macmillan, 1982), pg. 3.

2. *Attack from the Spirit World*, (Wheaton, IL: Tyndale House, 1973), pp. 203, 204.

CHAPTER 2 FOUNDATIONAL ISSUES

3. Timothy M. Warner, *Spiritual Warfare*, (Wheaton, IL: Crossway Books, 1991), pg. 24.

CHAPTER 3 DEMON POSSESSION

4. C. Fred Dickason, *Demon Possession & the Christian*, (Westchester, IL: Crossway Books, 1987).

5. Ibid.

CHAPTER 6 PRAYER, THE ULTIMATE WARFARE WEAPON

6. This story was distributed during a course on spiritual warfare while pursuing my Doctor of Ministry degree.

7. C. Fred Dickason, *Demon Possession & the Christian*, (Westchester, IL: Crossway Books, 1987), pp. 255, 256.

CHAPTER 7 POWER, TRUTH, AND AUTHORITY

8. John MacMillan, *The Authority of the Believer*, (Harrisburg, PA: Christian Publications, 1980).

CHAPTER 8 STEPS TO FREEDOM

9. Neil T. Anderson, *The Bondage Breaker*, (Eugene OR: Harvest House, 1990), pp. 237-247.

SELECTED BIBLIOGRAPHY

Amstuts, Wendell. *Exposing and Confronting Satanism*. Rochester, MN: National Counseling Resource Center, 1991.

Anderson, Neil. *The Bondage Breaker*. Eugene, OR: Harvest House, 1990.

________. *The Seduction of Our Children*. Eugene, OR: Harvest House, 1991.

________. *Victory Over the Darkness*. Ventura, CA: Regal Books, 1990.

________. *Walking Through the Darkness*. San Bernadino, CA: Here's Life Publishers, 1991.

Bernal, Dick. *Storming Hell's Brazen Gates*. Jubilee Christian Center, San Jose, 1989.

Bilheimer, Paul. *Destined for the Throne*. Ft. Washington, PA: Christian Literature Crusade, 1975.

Bounds, E.M. *The Essentials of Prayer*. Baker Book House, 1979.

Bryant, David. *With Concerts of Prayer*. InterVarsity, 1986.

Bubeck, Mark I. *The Adversary*. Chicago: Moody Press, 1974.

Bubeck, Mark I. *The Satanic Revival*. Here's Life, 1990.

________. *Overcoming the Adversary*. Chicago: Moody Press, 1984.

Chandler, Russell. *Understanding the New Age.* Word Publishing, 1988.

Christenson, Evelyn. *Battling the Prince of Darkness.* Wheaton: IL:Victor, 1990.

Dawson, John. *Taking Our Cities for God: How to Break Spiritual Strongholds.* Lake Mary, FL: Creation House, 1989.

deParrie, Paul. *Satan's Seven Schemes.* Brentwood, TN: Wolgemuth & Hyatt, 1991.

Dickason, C. Fred. *Demon Possession and the Christian.* Wheaton: Crossway Books, 1987.

Duewel, Wesley L. *Touch the World Through Prayer.* Grand Rapids: Zondervan/Francis Asbury Press, 1990.

________. *Mighty, Prevailing Prayer.* Grand Rapids: Zondervan/Asbury Press, 1990.

Graham, Billy. *Angels: God's Secret Agents.* Garden City, NY: Doubleday, 1975.

Green, Michael. *Exposing the Prince of Darkness.* Vine books, 1981.

Groothuis, Douglas. *Confronting the New Age.* Downers Grove: InterVarsity, 1988.

Hunter, Harold. *Simple Strategies for Spiritual Warfare.* Trinity Press, 1994.

Jacobs, Cindy. *Possessing the Gates of the Enemy.* Chosen Books, 1991.

Johnston, Jerry. *The Edge of Evil.* Dallas: Word, 1989.

Koch, Kurt E. *Demonology Past and Present.* Kregel Publishing, 1973.

Kraft, Charles. *Defeating Dark Angels.* Vine Books, 1992.

Larson, Bob. *Straight Answers on the New Age.* Nashville: Nelson, 1989.

Lewis, C.S. *The Screwtape Letters.* MacMillan, 1961.

MacMillan, John. *The Authority of the Believer.* Harrisburg: Christian Publications, 1980.

Michaelson, Johanna. *The Beautiful Side of Evil.* Eugene, OR: Harvest House Publications, 1982.

Montgomery, John Warwick. *Demon Possession.* Trinity Press, 1994.

Murphy, Ed. *The Handbook for Spiritual Warfare.* Thomas Nelson Publishers, 1992.

Piretti, Frank. *This Present Darkness.* Wheaton, IL: Crossway Books, 1986.

_______. *Piercing the Darkness.* Wheaton, IL: Crossway Books, 1989.

Porter, David. *Children at Risk: The Growing Risk of Bizarre Toys, Fantasy Games, TV, Movies, and Illegal Drugs.* Westchester, IL: Crossway, 1987.

Unger, Merrill F. *Demons in the World Today.* Wheaton: Tyndale House, 1976.

Wagner, Peter. *Engaging the Enemy.* Regal, 1991.

Wagner, Peter. *Wrestling with Dark Angels.* 1990.

Warner, Timothy M. *Spiritual Warfare*. Wheaton, IL: Crossway Books, 1991.

White, Thomas B. *The Believer's Guide to Spiritual Warfare*. Ann Arbor: Vine/Servant Publications, 1990.